NEW
English Adventure

Student's Book with Workbook

LEVEL 5

José Luis Morales
with Rhiannon Sarah Ball

© **Pearson Education do Brasil 2016.**

Copyright © 2016 Disney Enterprises, Inc. All rights reserved.
Pixar characters and artwork Copyright © Disney and Pixar.

All rights reserved; no part of this publication may be reproduced, stored in a retrieval system, or transmitted in any form or by any means, electronic, mechanical, photocopying, recording, or otherwise without the prior written permission of the Publishers.

First published 2016

New English Adventure Level 5 Student's book
ISBN 978-1-292-14139-8

Set in Frutiger Lt Pro (75 Black, 55 Roman, 45 light, 46 light italic)

Printed in Brazil

Head of Product- Pearson Brazil: Gabriela Diuana
Product Manager- Pearson Brazil: Marjorie Robles
Product Coordinator: Priscila Marconi
Design Coordinator: Cleber Carvalho
Authors: José Luis Morales with Rhiannon Ball
Editors: Rhiannon Ball, Priscila Marconi and Viviane Kirmeliene
Art and Design: Alto Contraste SP
Audio: Maximal Studio
Media Development: Estação Gráfica
MediaHub Manager: Fabiano Martins
Coordenação de licenciamento e ilustração: Maiti Salla e Carolina Meneghetti
Produção MediaHub: Tatiane Almeida, Maricy Queiroz, Alberto Rodrigues, Rebeca Fiamozzini e Sandra Sebastião
Fotógrafo: Alexandre Schneider
Locações: Escola Aldeia dos Pandavas e Quadra de tênis Vertical
Ilustrações: Comicup, Eduardo Borges

Pearson Education Brazil would like to thank Gisele Aga for her contribution during the development of the series.

Pearson Education Brazil would like to thank Gisele Aga for her contribution during the development of the series.

Student's Book
LEVEL 5

Contents	page
Hello	2
1. What are you good at?	6
2. There is a place for you and me	14
3. We have math on Monday	22
4. What's the matter?	30
5. My brother is younger than me	38

Contents	page
6. What do meerkats eat?	46
7. When I was five…	54
8. Once upon a time…	62
Happy Birthday	70
Happy Easter	71
Earth Day	72
Workbook	73

Go to https://newenglishadventure.pearson.com.br/ or https://ensino.pearson.com.br/suporte
and download Multi-Rom to access audio content and others

HELLO

1 Listen, read and say.

Hi! I'm Katy. School starts today.

It's time for school, it's **Monday**.
I have my **backpack**.
I have my **books**.
It's time for school. School starts today.
It's Saturday. It's Sunday.
No books. No class.
It's the weekend.
I don't have school today.

2 Read and say again. Change the words in purple.

1. TUESDAY

2. THURSDAY

3. WEDNESDAY

4. FRIDAY

Hello: *I'm ...*, days of the week, classroom objects.

3 Listen and read.

4 Look, ask and answer.

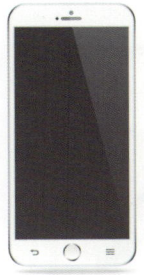

Hello: Greetings, Introductions, *How old are you? I'm (ten). Are you (in class 5B)? Do you have (a cell phone)? Yes, I do. / No, I don't.*

5 Listen and read. Then say.

6 Look, match and write. Then say.

Thanks.   Please.   Sorry!   Excuse me.

Hello: *Please, Thanks, Excuse me* and *Sorry*.

7 Listen and read.

Look at my pets. I love animals. I have a cat and a rabbit, but I don't have a fish or a dog. My favorite animals are rabbits. My rabbit is black and white.

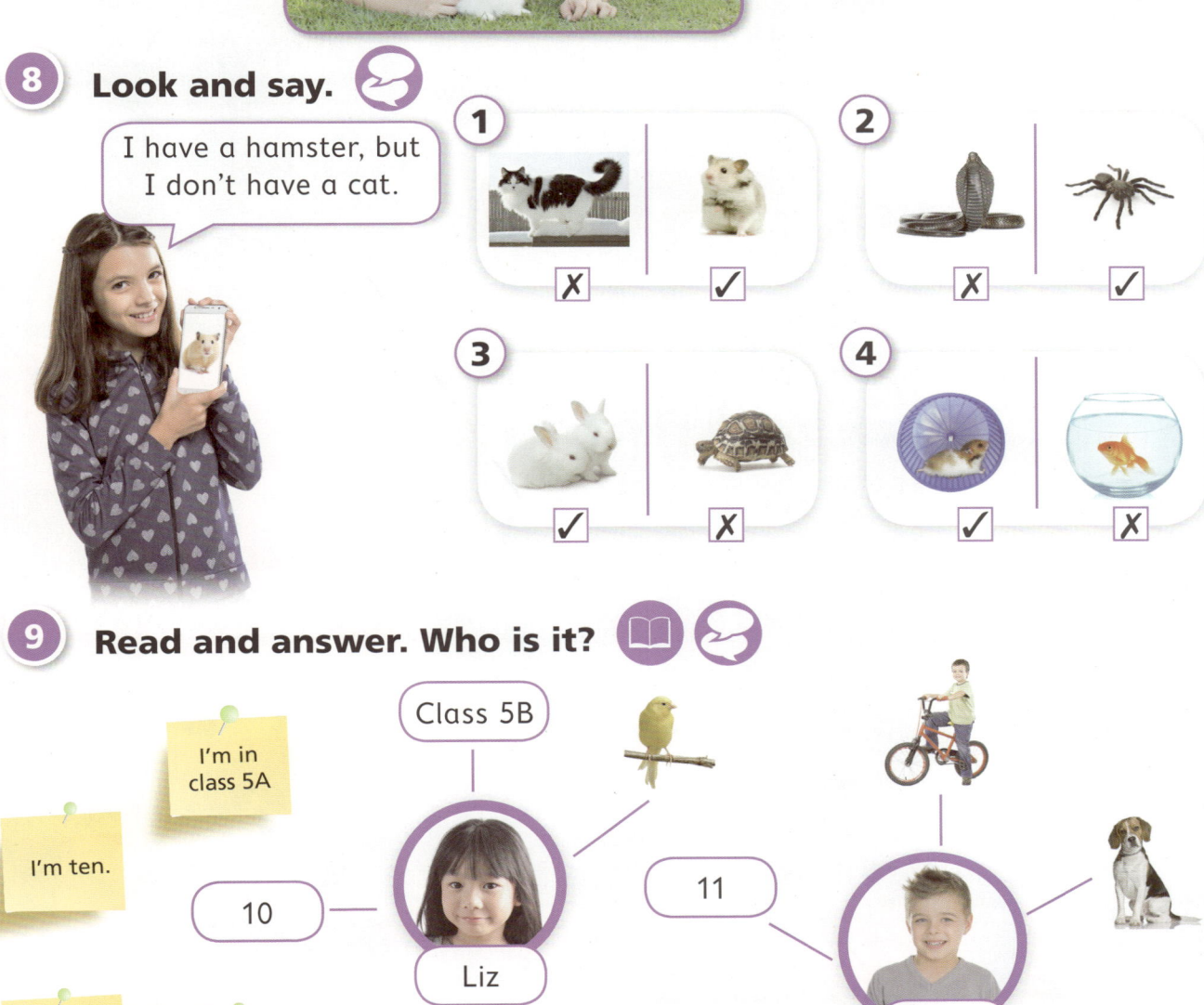

8 Look and say.

I have a hamster, but I don't have a cat.

1. ✗ ✓
2. ✗ ✓
3. ✓ ✗
4. ✓ ✗

9 Read and answer. Who is it?

Class 5B
I'm in class 5A
I'm ten.
10
Liz
11
Brad
I have a new bike.
My favorite animal is a bird.
Class 5A

10 Now say about you.

I have ..., but I don't have ...
My favorite animals are ...

Hello: *I have a (cat), but I don't have a (rabbit). My favorite animals are (rabbits).*

5

UNIT 1 What are you good at?

1 Look at the picture, then ask and answer.

1 What movie is this scene from?
2 What can you see?
3 What are they doing?
4 Can you remember any words for free time activities?

Opener: *Chicken Little*

2 Look, read and listen.

- Hi, Steve! Where are you?
- Hi, Katy! I'm at Sportsworld with Jake.
- What are you doing?
- We're playing tennis. Nina's here too. She's running. Do you want to come?

3 Read, look and find. Who's speaking?

1. I'm talking to Katy.
2. I'm running.
3. I'm playing tennis with Steve.
4. I'm calling Steve.

4 Listen and read.

My favorite sport is swimming. I like swimming in the sea, but I don't like playing volleyball on the beach. I like playing tennis, but I don't like dancing. Oh, and I like climbing, too!

Vocabulary: *What are you doing? I'm (playing tennis). I like (swimming), but I don't like (playing tennis). My favorite (sport) is (swimming).*

5 What do you like doing? Check (✓) or cross (✗). Then say.

6 What do they like doing? Look and say.

7 Listen, read and answer.

It's Wednesday afternoon. I'm playing soccer with my friends at school. We're on the school team. My best friend is running and kicking the ball. He's good at soccer. I'm good at playing soccer, too. It's my favorite sport.

1 What is Steve's friend doing?
2 What does Steve like doing?
3 What is Steve good at?

Skills: *dancing, kicking the ball, painting, playing badminton, playing soccer, playing tennis, reading, cycling, running, swimming, climbing, kitesurfing.*

GRAMMAR

What are you doing?	I'm	swimming. playing (soccer). cycling. snorkeling. running. climbing. reading. painting. dancing. kite surfing.
What do you like doing?	I like	
What are you good at?	I'm good at	

8 Read and match.

1 What are you good at?
2 Are you playing soccer?
3 What do you like doing?
4 Are you good at cycling?
5 What are you doing?

A I like singing.
B I'm talking on the phone.
C I'm good at singing.
D Yes, I'm playing soccer.
E No, I'm not good at cycling.

9 Look and play. What are you good at?

I'm good at playing soccer.

I'm not good at swimming.

heads    tails

A	
playing soccer	reading
singing	cycling
running	cooking
flying a kite	playing tennis
climbing	painting
swimming	playing volleyball

B	
listening to music	swimming
talking on the phone	flying a kite
climbing	reading
flying a kite	cooking
playing soccer	playing volleyball
singing	reading

Grammar: *What are you good at? I'm good at (singing). What do you like doing? I like (playing soccer). What are you doing? I'm (reading).*

10 **Read and say.**

11 **Tongue Twister! Listen and repeat.**

Story: *Are you good at (fixing things)? It's flying! I guess I'm not good at (fixing things).*

READY FOR LIFE

UNIT 1

12 Listen and read. Then number and write.

1 I'm good at climbing. I like playing soccer and volleyball, but I don't like painting. I think cooking is fun.

2 I like the gym, but I don't like playing tennis. I'm good at ballet. I think it's great.

3 I like studying English, but I don't like painting. I'm good at singing in English. I have lots of friends in the USA.

4 I'm not good at swimming, but I'm good at painting. I love reading and listening to music.

 Brad: _____

 Melissa: _____

 Donna: _____

 Adam: _____

13 Project: Make a video about you.

I like cycling and dancing. I love swimming and I'm good at running.

I like …
I love …
I'm good at … .

Ready for life: *We are all special.*

REVIEW 1

1 **Read and say. Then write in your notebook.**

"I like dancing, but I don't like singing."

🙂	☹️
dancing	swimming
playing tennis	climbing
cycling	kite surfing
painting	running
reading	snorkeling

2 **Match and say.**

1 What are you doing?

2 Are you good at singing?

3 What do you like doing?

4 What's your favorite animal?

A dog.

I love snorkeling.

I'm listening to music.

Yes, I am.

3 **Change the blue words in Activity 2, then ask and answer.**

Review 1

12

OUR WORLD

NIAGARA FALLS

Look at the photo. Can you see the waterfall? It's very big! This is Niagara Falls. It is in the USA and in Canada. There is a bridge between the two countries. At Niagara Falls there are lots of big and beautiful waterfalls. You can visit the falls by boat, by hot-air balloon and by helicopter. You can also see the falls from a tower. The tower is next to the river.

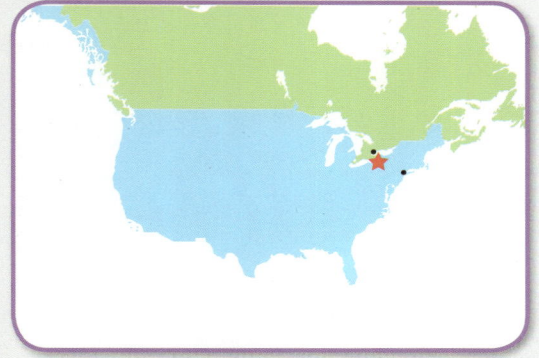

There are other things to do at Niagara Falls, too. You can do different sports in the snow, like snowboarding. Some people like riding snowmobiles too. ✈

Our World 1: Niagara Falls.

UNIT 2
There is a place for you and me

1 Look at the picture, then ask and answer.

1 What movie is this scene from?
2 What can you see?
3 Can you remember words for places in a city?

Opener: *Atlantis*

2 Look, read and listen.

3 Read and answer.

Steve lives at 12 Exeter Drive, in Turner.

1 Where does Nina live?
2 Where does Jake live?
3 Where does Katy live?
4 Where do you live?

2 Acton Avenue

18 Kingsman Close

Apartment 2, Rose Court

4 Match the names to the places and number. Then say.

1 drugstore   2 movie theater   3 park   4 supermarket   5 library   6 café

Vocabulary: *Is this your (cell phone)? Is that your (racket)? That's my (racket). Where do you live? (Steve) lives at (11) (Exeter Drive), in (Turner).*

5 Who is speaking? Read and write N for Nina and J for Jake.

There are stores. ☐
There are movie theaters. ☐
There are cafés. ☐
There are wild animals. ☐
There are forests. ☐
There are waterfalls. ☐

6 Ask and answer.

What do you like? The country or the town?

I like the country. There are forests and waterfalls.

7 Listen and circle T for true and F for false.

1 Jake is calling Katy. T / F
2 Steve invites Katy to go to the movies. T / F
3 Katy likes Adam Sandler. T / F
4 Katy can go to the movies tonight. T / F

Skills: *Do you like the (country)? Yes, there are (forests) and (waterfalls).*

UNIT 2

8 Listen and check (✓). Then say. CD 1.13

1 How much is this? It's …

 $4  $7  $2

2 How much are these? They're …

 $9  $19  $11

9 Ask and answer.

How much is this?

It's $20.

 $1    $3    $18

 $79    $17    $30

GRAMMAR

How much	is	this/that?
It's	twenty dollars.	
How much	are	these/those?
They're	thirty dollars.	

How much is this?

It's twenty dollars.

How much are these?

They're thirty dollars.

Grammar: *How much is this? It's (twenty) dollars. How much are these? They're (thirty) dollars.*

17

10 Read and say.

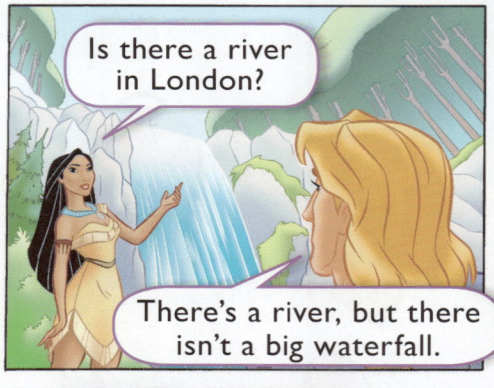

11 Tongue Twister! Listen and repeat.

Story: : *Where do you live? Is there a (river)? There are (houses and roads). Who's here?*

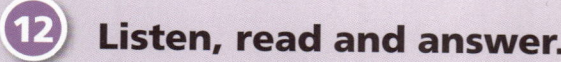

READY FOR LIFE

UNIT 2

12 Listen, read and answer.

I'm Julie. I live in the country and I love it. Every day, I go for a walk with my dog in the mountains. I listen to the birds. Buddy, my dog, runs and plays a lot. There is a beautiful waterfall and I can see wild animals. It's so cool.

I'm Noah. I live in the town. After school, my friends and I go skateboarding on the streets. There are movie theaters and stores. My family and I like to visit these places on the weekends. I love my town.

1 What does Julie do? And Noah?
2 Do you live in the country or in the town?
3 What do you like about where you live?

13 Project: Make a poster of your home town.

Ready for life: *I love my town!*

REVIEW 2

1 Look, read and answer.

2 Order the dialogue.

◯ How much are the tickets?
◯ I live in Turner.
◯ They're $8.
① Where do you live, Kevin?
◯ Yes, there is a movie theater.
◯ Is there a movie theater in Turner?

3 Match. Then write in your notebook.

1. How much is it?
2. There is
3. There are
4. How much are they?
5. I live in

A. a drugstore.
B. waterfalls in the country.
C. It's $20.
D. a town.
E. They're $22.

Review 2

OUR WORLD

THE MYSTERY OF LOCH NESS

Do you recognize the monster in the picture? That's the Loch Ness monster, and many people say that it lives in a loch in Scotland. A loch is a lake, and there are lots of them in Scotland. Loch Ness is in the north of Scotland and it is very big. The water is very dark and very deep. It is very cold too, so it is dangerous to go swimming in Loch Ness.

Loch Ness is very famous now, so there are lots of stores, restaurants and hotels in the town near it. Lots of tourists visit the area every year, and many of them look for the Loch Ness monster so they can take a photo of it! What about you, do you believe there is a monster in Loch Ness?

UNIT 3
We have math on Monday

1 Look at the picture, then ask and answer.

1 What movie is this scene from?
2 What can you see?
3 Can you remember any words about school?

Opener: *Monsters University*

2 Look, read and listen.

"Oh no! It's eight fifteen!"

"There's no cereal for breakfast. Typical!"

"Sorry!"

"Oh no! Please stop!"

Time	Monday	Tuesday	Wednesday	Thursday	Friday
9.00	English	Science	History	Math	English
11.30	Music	Geography	English	Math	English
12.30	L	U	N	Science	Math
2.15	Science	English	Music	English	PE
3.15	PE	Computer Science	Math	English	

"We're late! Where's our class?"

"Hmm, it's Wednesday. We have history at nine o'clock."

"You're late! Go to class!"

"Sorry, sir! Quick, let's go!"

3 Read and answer.

1 What day is music?
2 What time is lunch?
3 What days do Nina and Katy have math?
4 What time is PE on Friday?
5 What time is it right now?

Vocabulary: *You're late! We have (history) on Monday at (nine)(o'clock). (Science) is at (two)(fifteen).*

4 Listen and answer.

It's eleven fifteen.

1C.

It's three twenty.

2D.

5 Read the schedule on page 23. Then ask and answer.

What's your favorite subject? When and what time is it?

My favorite subject is on Thursday at two fifteen. What is it?

6 Look, ask and answer.

A: What do you need?
B: I need my paints.
A: When do you have it?
B: I have it at 10:15 on Tuesdays.
A: Is it art?
B: Yes, it is!

Skills: *When do you have (PE)? I have (PE) at (nine)(o'clock) on (Wednesday). What's your favorite subject?*

UNIT 3

7 Listen and repeat. CD 1.18

Good days

1. I get up at seven o'clock.

2. I get dressed at seven fifteen.

3. I have breakfast at seven thirty.

4. I take the bus at seven forty-five.

8 Read and answer. What time is it?

Bad days

1. Oh no! It's late!

2. Where are my pants?

3. That's my sandwich!

4. Oh no. Wait!

GRAMMAR

What time do you	get up get dressed have breakfast take the bus		?
I	go to school have lunch do homework go to bed	at	… o'clock. … fifteen. … thirty. … forty five. … fifty.

9 Look and choose. Then write in your notebook.

My ideal day
I get up at …
I go to …
I go by …
In the afternoon, I …
I go to bed at …

Grammar: *What time do you (get up)? I (get up) at (7 o'clock).*

25

10 **Read and say.**

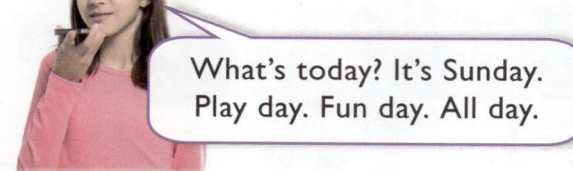

- Wake up, Goofy!
- What time is it?
- It's five o'clock in the morning.
- But it's dark outside.
- Let's clean the tent.
- Is it breakfast time?
- Yes, it's time for breakfast now. Here you are.
- Is that all?
- Let's share, Pluto...
- What about the meat?

11 **Tongue Twister! Listen and repeat.**

- What's today? It's Sunday. Play day. Fun day. All day.
- What's today? It's Sunday. Play day. Fun day. All day.

Story: *What time is it? Let's clean the tent. Breakfast time. Is that all?*

26

READY FOR LIFE

12 Listen, read and answer.

School is different all over the world. In the UK, the first class is in September, but in Australia it is in January. When is your first class of the year?

I'm Claude. I live in France. We don't have school on Wednesdays, but we study on Saturday. I don't wear a uniform. We start school at 8:00 a.m. Our vacation is in July and August.

I'm Maria. I'm from Uruguay. My uniform is blue and white. School starts at 8:30 a.m. and finishes at 5:00 p.m. We can have breakfast, lunch and dinner at school! We have vacation in January and February.

1 Do you prefer school in France or Uruguay? Why?
2 What time do you go to school?
3 Do you wear a uniform?
4 When are your school vacations?

13 Project: Make a poster about your school.

WELCOME TO TURNER ELEMENTARY SCHOOL

This is our schedule.

This is a classroom.

This is the library.

This is our soccer team.

This is our art class.

These are our teachers.

Ready for life: *School Life*

REVIEW 3

1 Look and say. Then write in your notebook.

I don't go to school by _____.

I get up at _____.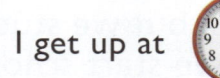

I am good at _____.

I have a _____.

My favorite subject is _____.

2 Look and say. What subjects does Steve have today? Write in your notebook.

3 Ask and answer.

What time do you wake up?

I wake up at 7 o'clock.

1 What time do you get up?
2 How do you go to school?
3 What are you good at?
4 What do you like doing on the weekend?

Review 3

OUR WORLD

LIVING AND LEARNING NEAR THE NORTH POLE

Welcome to Longyearbyen School. It's the first day of class and it's windy and very cold. Longyearbyen is a small village between the North Pole and Norway. There are tall mountains with snow and glaciers in the region, but there aren't any fields or forests. There are polar bears, reindeer and seals.

The children hats, gloves, sweaters, jackets and boots. Today they are riding bikes. It's September and there isn't any snow. December, January and February is very cold. There is snow and ice. The children and the teachers come to school on snowmobiles or dog sleds. At Longyearbyen School children have math, language, history and science.

This is an amazing part of the world. It's always dark in winter and it's always light in summer.

Our World 3: Living and learning near the North Pole.

UNIT 4 What's the matter?

1 Look at the picture, then ask and answer.

1 What movie is this scene from?
2 What can you see?
3 How is she feeling?
4 Can you remember words to describe feelings?

Opener: *Mulan*.

2 Look, read and listen.

3 Read and complete.

> toothache   soccer game   earache   cold   headache

1 Jake has a _____ and an _____.
2 He doesn't have a _____.
3 Katy thinks he has a _____.
4 Jake has a _____ this weekend.

4 What are Katy's suggestions for Jake? Look and match.

1 See   bed.
2 Go   the nurse.
3 Go to   home.

Vocabulary: *What's the matter? I have a (headache).*

31

5 Look, match and write the letter.

  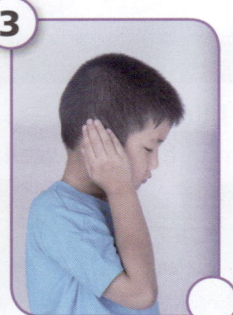  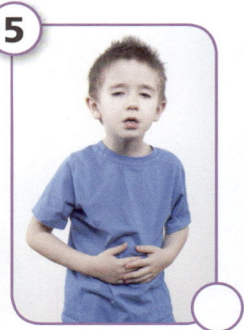

A a headache **D** a broken leg
B a cold **E** a broken arm
C a stomachache **F** an earache

6 Look at Activity 5. Then ask and answer.

Picture 1. What's the matter?

She has a broken leg.

7 Listen. Then answer. What can Jake do now? What can Jake do when he is better? Write in your notebook. CD 1.22

  Always have a healthy breakfast.

  Have hot tea with lemon and honey.

  Eat a lot of oranges. They have vitamin C.

  Do exercise.

 Drink water.

  Go to bed early.

Skills: *What's the matter? Oh no! (He) has a (broken arm). What can I do? You can do exercise.*

UNIT 4

8 Listen, read and repeat. Then play.

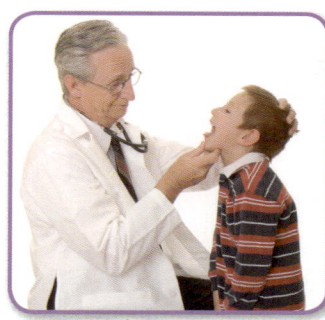

A: What's the matter?
B: I have a sore throat.
A: Do you have a cough?
B: Yes, I do. What can I do?
A: You can drink hot water and lemon.

GRAMMAR

I / You	have	a cold. a cough. a sore throat. a headache. a broken leg. a broken arm. an earache. a stomachache. the flu.
She / He / It	has	

What's the matter?

I have an earache.

9 Look and write. Then ask and answer.

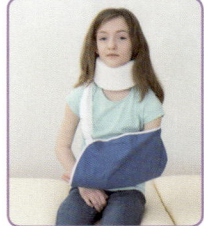

What's the matter?

She has a broken arm.

1 *She has a broken arm*.

4 _____.

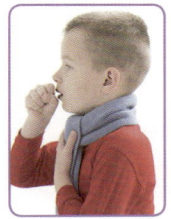

2 _____.

3 _____.

5 _____.

Grammar: *What's the matter? I have (a broken arm). He/She has (the flu). You/We/They have (an earache).*

33

10 Read and say.

11 Tongue Twister! Listen and repeat.

Story: *He's not very well. Have a drink of water. That's better!*

READY FOR LIFE

UNIT 4

12 Listen, read and answer. Circle T for true or F for false.

In some countries, hospitals are very different. They do not have beds or medicine. People that are sick can't get better.
Some doctors travel to these countries to help. They take medicine and teach the local doctors. They help the children who have bad coughs and broken legs or arms. They give comics and books to the children in the hospital. These doctors are very special.

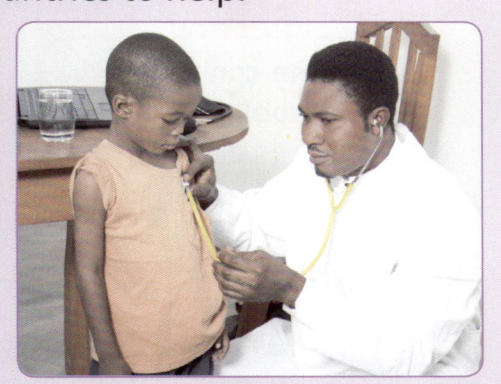

1 Hospitals are the same in all countries.   T / F
2 Some doctors go to different countries.   T / F
3 The doctors don't teach.   T / F
4 The children aren't sick.   T / F
5 The doctors take video games.   T / F

13 Work with a partner. Answer the questions.

1 Who looks after you when you are sick?
2 Do you like reading comics and books when you're sick?
3 Do you go to school when you're sick?

14 Project: Design a get-well e-card for a friend.

Think about:

What does the card say?
What picture is in it?
Is it animated?

Ready for life: Brave doctors

35

REVIEW 4

1 Look and say.

She can't play volleyball. She has …

He can't walk to school. He has …

She can't sing. She has …

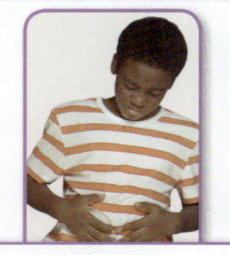

He can't have lunch. He has …

She doesn't feel well. She has …

He can't go to school. He has …

2 Match.

1. You can drink hot water and lemon.
2. I'm not feeling well.
3. I have an earache.
4. I can't eat now.
5. You're late. Hurry!
6. Can you take me to school, Mom? I can't walk.

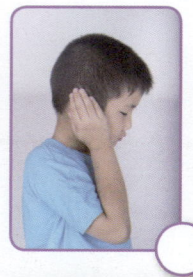

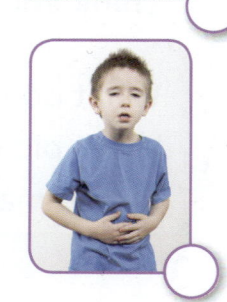

OUR WORLD

RAINY CHERRAPUNJI AND THE LIVING ROOT BRIDGES

The town of Sohra, or Cherrapunji, is in northeast India. It's always rainy in this part of the world. It has a Guinness World Record! There are beautiful green fields, rivers, waterfalls and forests in Cherrapunji. Plants and trees love the rain! In the forests there are very large, green trees. They have very long roots. The roots make great bridges. Now Sohrans can cross the rivers. Look at the photo. That's a living bridge! It is probably hundreds of years old. A lot of people can walk on the bridge at the same time. It is very strong.

Our World 4: Rainy Cherrapunji and the living root bridges.

UNIT 5
My brother is younger than me

1 Look at the picture, then ask and answer.

1 What movie is this picture from?
2 What can you see?
3 What do they look like? Are they the same or different?
4 Can you remember the words to describe people?

Opener: *The Jungle Book*

2 Look, read and listen.

- Do you have brothers or sisters?
- Yes, I do. I have a sister and two brothers. Do you?
- Yes, a brother. I'm ten and he's nine.
- Look, here's a picture of us.
- But he's taller than you! Oh, sorry!
- That's OK. He's younger, but he's taller than me.
- It's his birthday soon.
- That's a coincidence. It's my birthday in April, too!

3 Read and answer. Circle T for true and F for false.

1 Jake has a brother. T / F
2 His brother's birthday is in June. T / F
3 Nina's birthday is in April. T / F
4 Jake is taller than his brother. T / F

Vocabulary: *He's (younger) than me. My birthday is in (April).*

4 Listen and say. Then ask and answer. CD 1.27

When's Nina's birthday?

It's in April.

Nina → April
Katy → May
Steve → August
Jake → December

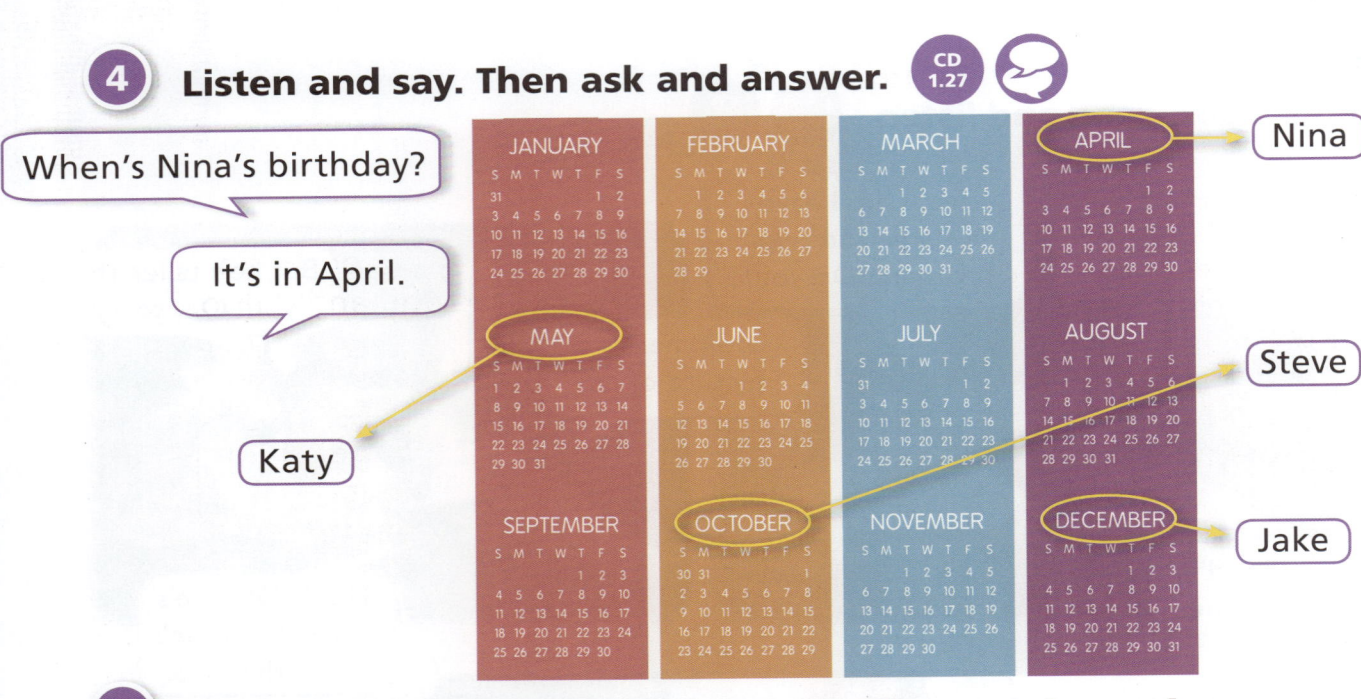

5 Look at the people in the pictures. Then read, number and say.

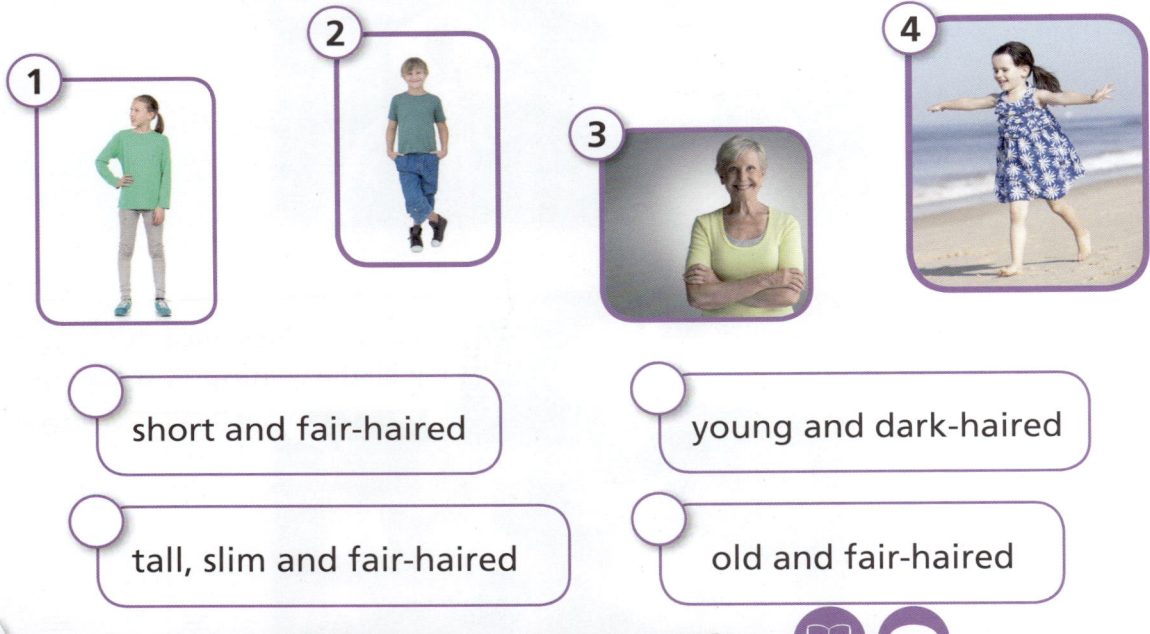

1 2 3 4

- short and fair-haired
- young and dark-haired
- tall, slim and fair-haired
- old and fair-haired

6 Look and read. Then say the opposite.

This is my brother, Joe. He's younger than me. He's shorter than me. He is fair-haired. He isn't faster than me!

7 Work with a partner. Talk about someone in your family.

Skills: When's (Nina's) birthday? It's in (April). Physical appearance: tall, short, dark-haired, fair-haired, young, old, slim

UNIT 5

8 Read and say the name.

"I'm longer than Mowgli and Baloo."

"I'm bigger than everybody!"

9 Ask and answer.

"Is Mowgli taller than Baloo?"
"Yes, he is."

"Is Hathi stronger than Shanti?"
"No, he isn't."

| Is | Mowgli
Shere Khan
Baloo | shorter
taller
stronger
bigger | than | Kaa?
Hathi?
Bagheera? |

GRAMMAR

| Is | my
your
his
her
our
their | brother
mother
father
sister
teacher
friend | shorter
older
younger
stronger
taller
smaller | than | my
your
his
her | sister?
friend?
father?
brother? |

| Yes, | he | is. |
| No, | she | isn't. |

Grammar: *Is (Mowgli) shorter than (Baloo)? Yes, (he) is. No, (he) isn't.*

10 **Read and say.**

Look, Minnie. He's taller than Mickey.

Oh look, Goofy. There's Mickey!

His legs are longer.

And he is stronger than Mickey!

Go, Mickey!

But nobody is faster than Mickey!

11 **Tongue Twister! Listen and repeat.**

A loud brown mouse found a round cloud.

A loud brown mouse found a round cloud.

Story: *His legs are longer. He is stronger. Go, Mickey!*

READY FOR LIFE

UNIT 5

12 Listen, read and answer.

These are photos of 'twins'. Twins are brothers and sisters with the same birthday. They can be 'identical' or 'fraternal'. Identical twins look the same. They have the same color hair and eyes. They aren't shorter or taller. Fraternal twins are different. They can be a boy and a girl. Sometimes they look different, too. The boy can be fair-haired and the girl can be dark-haired, for example. Do you know any twins?

1 Are there different types of twins?
2 Can twins be boys and girls?
3 Can one twin be taller than the other twin?
4 Do you have friends who are twins? Are they identical?

13 Project: Make a poster.

Find out about famous twins.

Are they identical or fraternal twins?
Are they similiar or different?
Tell your classmates about them.

Ready fot life: Twins

43

REVIEW 5

1. Read and write the names of the surfboards.

I love surfing. I have three surfboards! They have the names of famous islands, Maui, Fiji and Bali. Fiji is taller than Maui. Fiji is shorter than Bali.

2. When are their birthdays? Read and say.

My birthday is in April.
Nina

I'm six months younger than Bill.
Trish

I'm older than Leo, but a month younger than Nina.
Lucy

I'm nine months younger than Nina.
Leo

I'm two months older than Nina.
Bill

3. In your notebook, write about your brother, sister, or a friend. Then say.

I'm older / younger than my …
His / Her birthday is in …
He / She is … than me.

Review 5

OUR WORLD

THE SAHARA

The Sahara is a large desert in northern Africa. It's bigger than the United States of America. There are sand dunes, scorpions and camels, but there aren't hippos, elephants or giraffes. There aren't lakes, fields or waterfalls. It is very hot and there isn't a lot of water. The Sahara is very dry and very windy.

Look at the people in the photo. They are eating, drinking and resting. It's an oasis. They travel in the desert with their camels and tents. They stop to rest and drink water here.

It wasn't always hot and dry. It was a green forest in the past. It was rainy, hot and big. How do we know? There are caves and rocks with very old paintings in the Sahara region. The paintings show giraffes, buffalo, men and women. Can a forest change into a desert? Yes, it can. The consequences are scary. No more water, no more fields, no more animals, no more life.

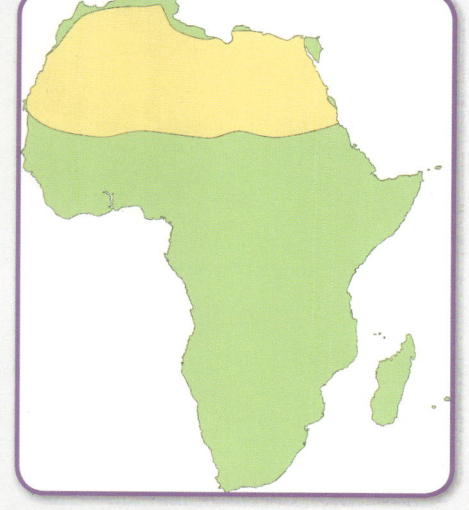

Our World 5: *The Sahara*

45

UNIT 6
What do meerkats eat?

1 **Look at the picture, then ask and answer.**

1 What movie is this scene from?
2 What can you see?
3 Can you remember the words for different animals?

Opener: *A Bug's life*

46

2 Look, read and listen.

OK. Research wild animals. Not pets or farm animals, please.

HOMEWORK
RESEARCH A WILD ANIMAL
DUE: MONDAY 13

Where do they live? What do they eat? Where do they sleep?

European bison are huge animals. They are 2 meters tall. These ones live in a forest in Poland. They eat grass and plants.

These are chimpanzees. They live in Africa. They live in forests and sleep in trees. They eat flowers, leaves, and fruit. Their favorite food is bananas.

These are meerkats. They live in the plains of Southern Africa. They eat insects, birds, and fruit.

3 Read and answer.

1 Can the children research cats or sheep for homework?
2 What do bison eat?
3 Where do chimpanzees sleep?
4 Where do meerkeats live?

4 Look and number. Then say.

1 cage   2 seeds   3 den   4 grass   5 meat   6 cave   7 plants

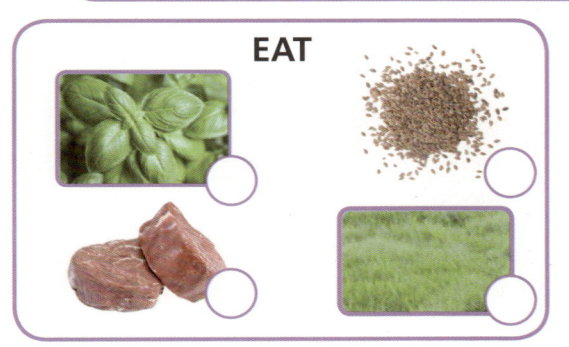

EAT

SLEEP

Vocabulary: *Where do (meerkats) (live)? What do (meerkats) eat? Wild animals.*

47

5 Read, write in your notebook and say.

	They live in	Their fur is	They eat	They sleep
Giant pandas	China	black and white	plants and bamboo shoots	In the trees
Brown bears	North America and Europe	brown	meat, plants and berries	in caves
Polar bears	the Arctic	white	meat	in dens

Giant pandas live in China. Their fur is black and white and they eat plants and bamboo shoots. They sleep under trees.

6 Play. Guess which bear your partner is talking about.

They're giant pandas.

They eat plants. They sleep under trees. They live in China.

Skills: (Giant pandas) live in China. They eat (bamboo shoots). Their fur is (black and white). They sleep (under trees). Wild animals.

7 Read, listen and answer.

Katy doesn't have a pet at home. She lives in an apartment. But she has two puppies, Billy and Belle. They are chow-chows. Their fur is white and their tongues are blue. They live in the country with Katy's grandparents. Katy visits them on weekends. They eat meat and rice and they sleep in comfortable kennels.

1 What are the dog's names?
2 Where do they live?
3 What do they eat?
4 Where do they sleep?

GRAMMAR

Where	do	bison chimpanzees giant pandas your pets	live	?	They	live	in forests. in the yard. in the house.
What	do	they	eat	?	They	eat	meat. plants. fruit. grass. seeds.
Where	do	they	sleep	?	They	sleep	in dens. in caves. in a basket. in a kennel. in a cage.

8 Ask and answer about these animals.

Grammar

49

9 **Read and say.**

1. The young ants are putting on a show about the grasshoppers.
   Oh, good! I love shows!

2. The grasshoppers are big and strong. They can jump a long way.

3. They fly here and eat our food!
   Where's our food? Give it to us.

4. The grasshoppers get angry when they don't get their food.
   What do angry grasshoppers do?

5. Die, ants!

6. Excuse me. When is dinner?
   Help! The grasshoppers are here!

7. The bugs run away.
   Come back. I'm not a grasshopper!

10 **Tongue Twister! Listen and repeat.** CD 1.32

On a gray day, the snake stays by the lake eating cake.

On a gray day, the snake stays by the lake eating cake.

Story: The grasshoppers are big and strong. They get angry.

READY FOR LIFE

UNIT 6

11 Listen, read and answer.

Yuck!

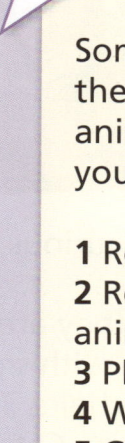

Some people don't like snakes, spiders or bugs. They think they are yucky! Zoophobia means that you are scared of animals. It's not good to be scared of animals. Here's what you can do to help:

1 Read about the animals you don't like.
2 Read a book with pictures of the animal.
3 Play with a toy animal.
4 Watch the animal on film.
5 Go to a pet center or zoo and look at the real animals.

1 What animals are people scared of?
2 What do you say when you don't like something?
3 What is zoophobia?
4 What can you do to help with zoophobia?

12 Project: Make a bookmark of a bug or an animal people don't like.

SPIDER

Ready for life: *Are you afraid of animals?*

REVIEW 6

1 **Read and answer. Do you prefer cats or hamsters? Why?**

A CAT OR A HAMSTER?

Hamsters are smaller than cats. They have soft fur and live in cages. They need fresh water to drink and a healthy diet. They eat seeds and insects, but they like vegetables and apples. Their teeth are small, but sharp. They like playing on their wheel and are very curious and friendly, but they don't like cats.

Cats have soft fur too, but they are bigger than hamsters. Cats love playing with small objects and sleeping on sofas and chairs. Their teeth and their nails are very sharp. Cats like fish and milk, but they usually eat special cat food with vitamins. Cats like hamsters … for lunch! Both cats and hamsters need a lot of love and care, but you can't have both.

2 **Read and decide: cats, hamsters or both? Write in your notebook.**

1 They have soft fur.
2 They need a healthy diet.
3 Their teeth are sharp.
4 They live in cages.
5 They like to eat hamsters.

3 **Read the text about dogs. Then choose an animal and write about it in your notebook.**

Dogs have soft fur.
They can be big or small.
They live in houses or gardens.
They sleep in kennels or on the couch.
They need lots of love.

OUR WORLD

THE AUSTRALIAN OUTBACK

Look at the picture. This is Uluru in Australia. It is also called Ayers Rock. Many people like visiting it in the evening to see the beautiful colors. For the Aboriginal people in Australia, Uluru is a very special place.

Uluru is in the Outback of Australia. The Outback is a very large area, but it doesn't have a specific location. Not many people live there, but there are lots of wild animals! You can find snakes, spiders and scorpions there. It rains a lot in the Outback and the temperatures are extreme. In June and July it is very cold, but in November and December it is very hot. There are different time zones in the Outback. This means the time is different in different places. The Outback covers a lot of Australia, but the Red Center is the most popular. Uluru is in the Red Center.

UNIT 7
When I was five...

1 **Look at the picture, then ask and answer.**

1 What movie is this scene from?
2 What can you see?
3 Can you describe the boy, the man and the bird?

Opener: *Up*

54

2 Look, read and listen.

Look! It's an old photo.

Is that you?

Aww!

Yes. I was five years old. I was small and slim and my hair was short. My eyes were smaller. I was happy and friendly. My pet was a puppy.

3 Read and answer. Circle T for true and F for false.

1 Nina was five years old in the photo.   T / F
2 She was small, but chubby.   T / F
3 Her hair was short.   T / F
4 She was happy.   T / F
5 Her pet was a kitten.   T / F

4 Look and read. Talk about Steve and Katy.

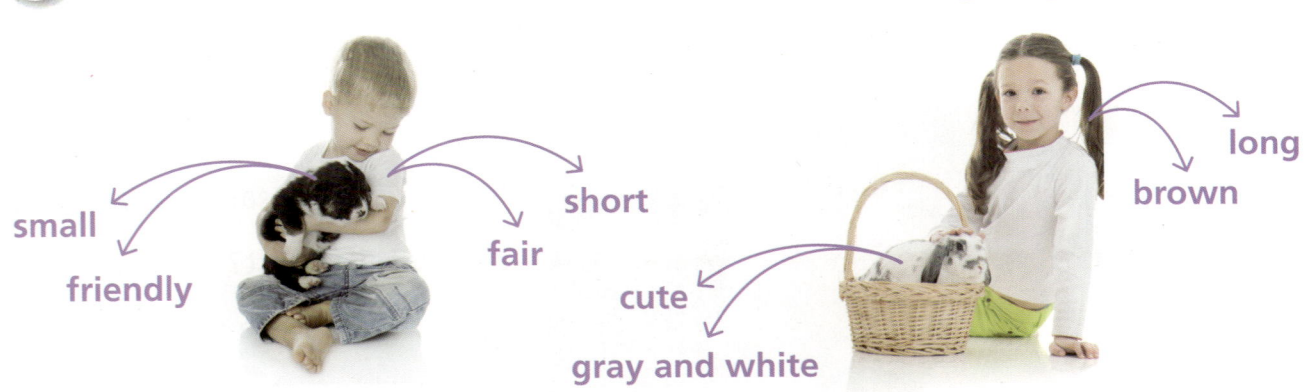

small
friendly
short
fair
cute
gray and white
long
brown

His hair was short. His dog was small.

Vocabulary: (She) was (five). (Her) (hair) was (long). (Her) (eyes) were (small). (Her) pet was a (puppy).

55

5 Read and say. In your notebook, write about Jake.

His

was
were

long / short / dark
small / big / brown
a soccer ball

6 Read, ask and answer.

Nina - Age 5 — 1m 10cm
Jake - Age 4 — 1m
Kate - Age 4 — 1m 03cm
Steve - Age 5 — 1m 13cm

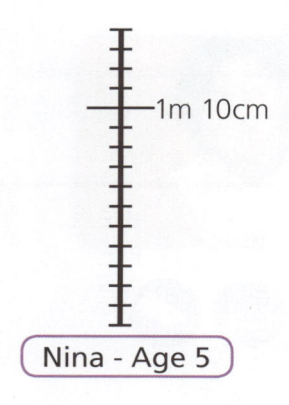

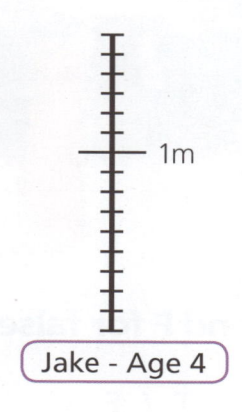

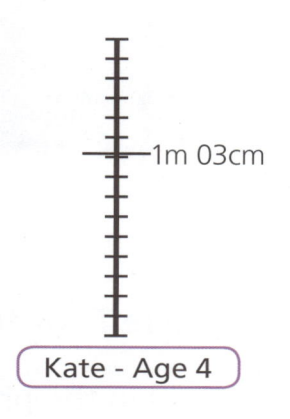

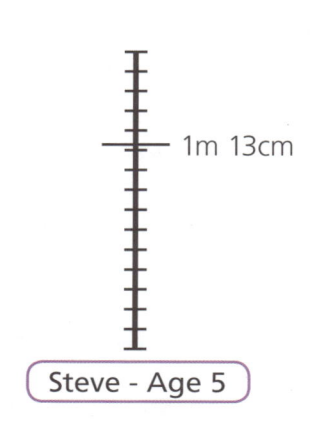

A: How old was Nina?
B: She was five.
A: How tall was she?
B: She was 1m 10 cm.

1 Who was taller at 5? Nina or Steve?
2 Who was shorter at 4? Katy or Jake?

7 Read, listen and answer.

This dinosaur was huge! Its body was ten meters long and it was four meters tall. Its claws were thirty-five centimeters long. They were big and sharp. It was a meat and fish eater. Its jaw was very strong.

1 Was the dinosaur a meat eater?
2 How tall was it?
3 How long were its claws?
4 Was its jaw strong?

Skills: How old was (Nina)? She was (five). How tall was (she)? She was (1 m 10 cm). (Steve) was (taller) than (Nina).

UNIT 7

8 Look at the picture. Ask and answer.

short   sad   young   tall
old   gray   happy

Was he happy?

Yes, he was.

GRAMMAR

Was	he/she	tall/short	?
Were	his/her	eyes	blue?

Yes, No,	he/she	was. wasn't.
Yes, No,	they	were. weren't.

How	tall	was	it	?
How	long	were	its	claws?

It	was	3 meters	tall.
They	were	35 centimeters	long.

9 Complete the dialogue. Then practice with a partner.

weren't   it   How long   Was   Yes   wasn't   Were

A: Look at this picture of my family. Guess which person was my grandpa?
B: OK. **1** _____ he tall?
A: No, he **2** _____.
B: **3** _____ his eyes blue?
A: No, they **4** _weren't_.
B: Was his hair brown?
A: Yes, **5** _____ was.
B: Hmm. **6** _____ was his hair?
A: It was very long.
B: Was this him?
A: **7** _____, it was. Good guess!

Grammar: *How (tall) was (he)? (He) was 1 m tall. Was (her hair) (long)? Yes, it was. / No, it wasn't.*

57

10 **Read and say.**

Look, Mickey! A dinosaur!

Wow! It's huge!

Oh Mickey, sleeping again... Let me get some popcorn.

Millions of years ago, there were huge dinosaurs on our planet.

Oh, no! It's here.

Just a dream...

What's the matter?

... a bad dream about a dinosaur.

Is Pluto your dinosaur?

Hahahaha...

11 **Tongue Twister! Listen and repeat.**

Poor dinosaur! Its claw's in the door. And it's sore!

Poor dinosaur! Its claw's in the door. And it's sore!

Story: *A huge dinosaur. Let me get some popcorn. A bad dream.*

58

UNIT 7

READY FOR LIFE

12 Listen, read and answer.

We can look at pictures of people when they were younger. But we can't look at dinosaurs! Scientists study dinosaurs to find out about them. They look at fossils. A fossil is a plant or animal inside a rock. Some fossils were on the planet millions of years ago! They can look at bones, too. The Baroyonyx dinosaur was ten meters long and it was four meters tall. Its claws were thirty-five centimeters long. Scientists know this because they look at the bones.

a fossil.

a baryonyx dinosaur.

1 Can we look at photos of dinosaurs?
2 When were fossils?
3 Was a Baryonyx a dinosaur?
4 How long was it?

13 Project: Make a short presentation about a dinosaur.

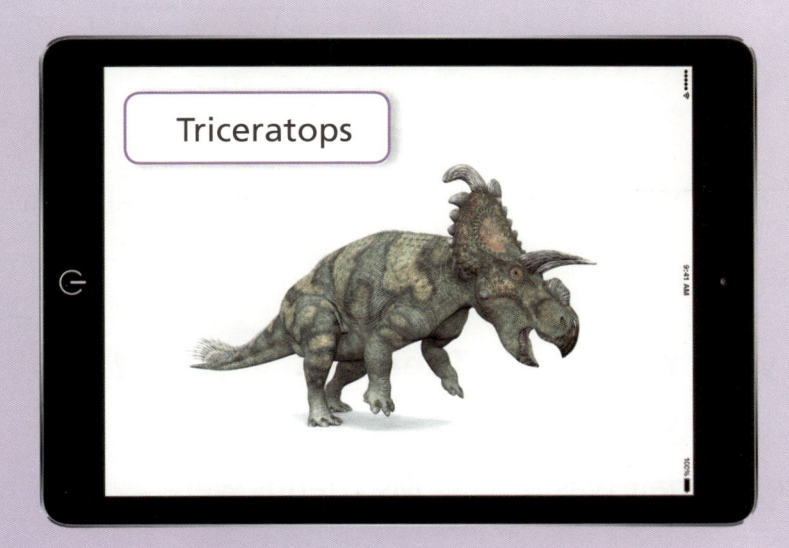

Triceratops

Ready for life: Animals of the past

59

REVIEW 7

1 Look, read and answer. Which dinosaur is it?

This was my pet dinosaur when I was five. The real dinosaur was heavy and its body was 12 meters long. It was 6 meters tall. Its tail wasn't very long, but its teeth and claws were long and sharp. There weren't spikes on its back, but it was very strong and scary.

1. Triceratops
2. Tyrannosaurus Rex

2 Look and guess. Then say.

Who/What was it?

What were they?

3 Write in your notebook. Then say.

When I was five, my hair was …

My friends were …

My toys were …

Review 7

OUR WORLD

KIRIBATI: A DISAPPEARING ISLAND?

Kiribati is a collection of small islands in the middle of the Pacific Ocean. Many years ago, there was space for everyone, but now there are lots of people on the islands. But this isn't the only change that people in Kiribati can see.

People say that the island is disappearing! This is because the level of the sea water is higher now, so the water enters into houses and buildings on the island. Some people build walls from rocks on the beaches, to protect their houses. This isn't a good solution because the seawater cleans the beaches and lakes. Now, there is trash and pollution in different places.

Can an island disappear? Some people say it is possible. This is very scary for the people of Kiribati. ✈

UNIT 8
Once upon a time...

1 Look at the picture, then ask and answer.

1 What movie is this scene from?
2 What can you see?
3 Can you describe Hercules and the monster?

Opener: *Hercules*

2 Look, read and listen. CD 1.38

Once upon a time there was a kingdom called Idyllia.

I am King Roderick of Idyllia.

And I am Queen Clarissa. Our people are scared.

The people were scared. There was a scary dragon in town. It was ten meters long and three meters tall. Its claws were strong and its ears were big.

The dragon is eating all our food and destroying our homes. There are fires in the town and in the forest. We need help.

A young man is looking and listening. His name is Phillip. He is clever.

Let's make a lot of noise!

That's a good idea. Everyone can help.

Look! The dragon doesn't like the church bells. His claws are on his ears.

The people of Idyllia clapped and cheered. They were happy and free again.

Thank you, young man. You're brave and clever.

3 Read and answer. Circle T for true and F for false.

1 The people of Idyllia were scared.   T / F
2 The dragon was ten meters tall.   T / F
3 The dragon likes noise.   T / F
4 Phillip was very clever.   T / F

4 Read and answer.

1 What was the name of the play?
2 What time was the play on November 9?
3 Was the play on on November 11?
4 What day was November 10?

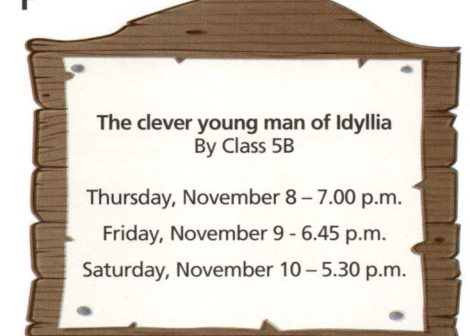

The clever young man of Idyllia
By Class 5B

Thursday, November 8 – 7.00 p.m.
Friday, November 9 - 6.45 p.m.
Saturday, November 10 – 5.30 p.m.

Vocabulary: *The people were (scared). Let's (make a lot of noise). You are (brave) and (clever).*

63

5 Look and number. Then say.

1 romance
2 adventure
3 magic and wizards
4 science fiction
5 history

What do you like to read?

I like books about …

6 Read and answer.

1 What books does she like?
2 Who is her favorite book about?
3 Was Cleopatra a heroine?
4 Was Cleopatra brave?
5 What was Cleopatra good at?

I like books about history. My favorite book is about Cleopatra. She was a queen in Egypt. She was very clever and beautiful. She was good at solving problems and looking after snakes.

7 Talk about your favorite story.

My favorite story is about …

He/She was a …

He/She was good at …

He/She was …

Skills: Arthur was famous for (his round table). Cleopatra was a (queen). (He) (was good at) (solving mysteries).

UNIT 8

8 Look and play. Invent a hero or heroine for a video game.

heads — tails

Toss a coin to start. Choose *He* or *She* and give him or her a name.

He's/She's …	twelve.	eleven.
He/She has …	X-Ray vision.	an invisibility helmet.
He/She lives in …	Tokyo.	London.
He/She likes/doesn't like …	running.	sailing.
He's/She's good at …	protecting people.	solving mysteries.
He/She can …	fly.	talk to animals.

GRAMMAR

| Was | he/she | clever | ? |
| Were | they | brave | ? |

| Yes/No, | he/she | was/wasn't. |
| Yes/No, | they | were/weren't. |

9 Write the questions. Then match.

1 the / princess / clever / Was / ?
_____

2 dragons / Were / scary / ?
_____

3 Hercules / Was / brave / ?
_____

4 handsome / the monster / Was / ?
_____

a Yes, they were.

b No, it wasn't.

c Yes, she was.

d Yes, he was.

Grammar: *Was (he/she) (clever)? Yes, he was. No, he wasn't. Were (you/ we/ they) (brave)? Yes, they were. No, they weren't.*

10 **Read and say.**

1. Hercules and Phil are in the forest.
   - Help! I was in the mountains. There's a terrible hydra there!
   - We are not scared of hydras!

2. They go to the bottom of the mountain.
   - It lives in the cave.

3. It's coming out! It's smaller than other hydras.
   - Is this it? I'm not scared of this little monster.

4. Get in the cage!

5. It was easy.
   - That's not the hydra.
   - What are you talking about?

6. There's the real hydra.

7. Phil throws the sword to Hercules.
   - You're the hero, Hercules. You fight this one!

11 **Tongue Twister! Listen and repeat.**

Never write a clever letter together!

Never write a clever letter together!

Story: Help! There's a terrible hydra. Is this is? It was easy. You're the hero.

READY FOR LIFE

UNIT 8

12 Listen, read and answer.

Today, we can read stories in books and online. But many years ago, there weren't books or computers! Look at these pictures. They are in caves in California. They are very old! In the pictures we can see birds, fish and people. There are deer and mountain lions, too. Some have arrows in their bodies. The pictures show stories about ancient heroes. There are also paintings in France, Spain, Africa, and the USA. We don't know anything about these artists and their stories. It is a mystery!

1 Where are the pictures?
2 Is there a museum or art gallery in your town?
3 What can you see there?

13 Project: Invent and write a picture story about a hero or heroine.

Once upon a time, there was a king. The king was brave ...

Ready for life: *Pictures tell stories*

67

REVIEW 8

1 Read and say. Then write in your notebook.

The dragon was in a field.

2 Change the blue words. Ask and answer.

1 castle
2 supermarket ✗
3 church
4 square ✗
5 fields
6 mountains ✗
7 forest

Was the dragon in the supermarket?

No, it wasn't.

Yes, it was.

Was the dragon in the castle?

3 Who is a famous real hero or heroine in your country? In your notebook, write about him or her. Then say.

Review 8

OUR WORLD

ANTARCTICA

Look at this picture of Antarctica. Can you believe that it is a desert? Antarctica is a desert because it doesn't rain a lot, and most of this rain is snow. Antarctica is the opposite end of the planet to the North Pole in the Arctic Circle, so you can find the South Pole in Antarctica. It is also very big — bigger than Europe!

Many years ago, there were forests in Antarctica, but not now. It is very difficult to live there, because it is very cold and windy. Also, there is a lot of ice. In fact, 90% of all of the ice on Earth is in Antarctica. Antarctica also has 70% of the planet's water. That's a lot of water! Because of all this, there are lots of sea animals in Antarctica, like penguins and whales. But there are no land animals. What do you think it is like to visit Antarctica?

Our World 8: Antartica

HAPPY BIRTHDAY

1 Listen, read and say. CD 1.41

1 birthday cake
2 birthday party
3 candles
4 invitation
5 presents

2 Listen and answer. CD 1.42

1 When is Katy's birthday?
2 What time is the party?
3 Who is Katy inviting?

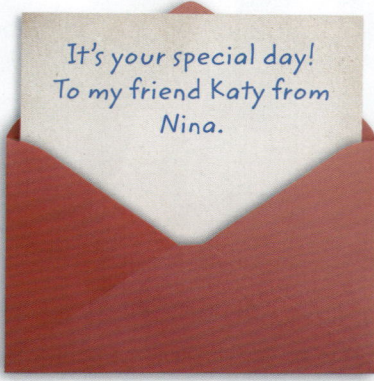

It's my birthday.

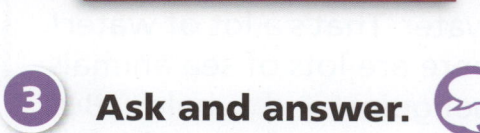

It's your special day!
To my friend Katy from Nina.

YOU ARE SPECIAL, KATY!
HAPPY BIRTHDAY.
Steve

3 Ask and answer.

1 When is your birthday?
2 Do you have a party?
3 What do you do at your party?
4 How many candles are on your cake this year?

Happy Birthday

HAPPY EASTER

1 Listen and read. Circle T for true and F for false.

1 Bunnies aren't symbols of Easter.
T / F

2 Easter is in March or April.
T / F

3 We decorate a tree at Easter.
T / F

4 We eat chocolate eggs at Easter.
T / F

5 We paint eggs at Easter.
T / F

2 Read and match.

1 On Easter Monday, many American families get together and have an Easter Egg Roll.
2 The children roll their eggs on the lawn in the garden.
3 The first egg that crosses the line is the champion!

3 Listen and check (✔).

1 What was Steve's present from his grandma?

A ◯ a rabbit   B ◯ chocolate soccer balls   C ◯ chocolate rabbit

2 How many chocolate eggs does he have?

A ◯ one   B ◯ two   C ◯ three

Happy Easter

71

EARTH DAY

1 Listen and read. Circle T for true and F for false.

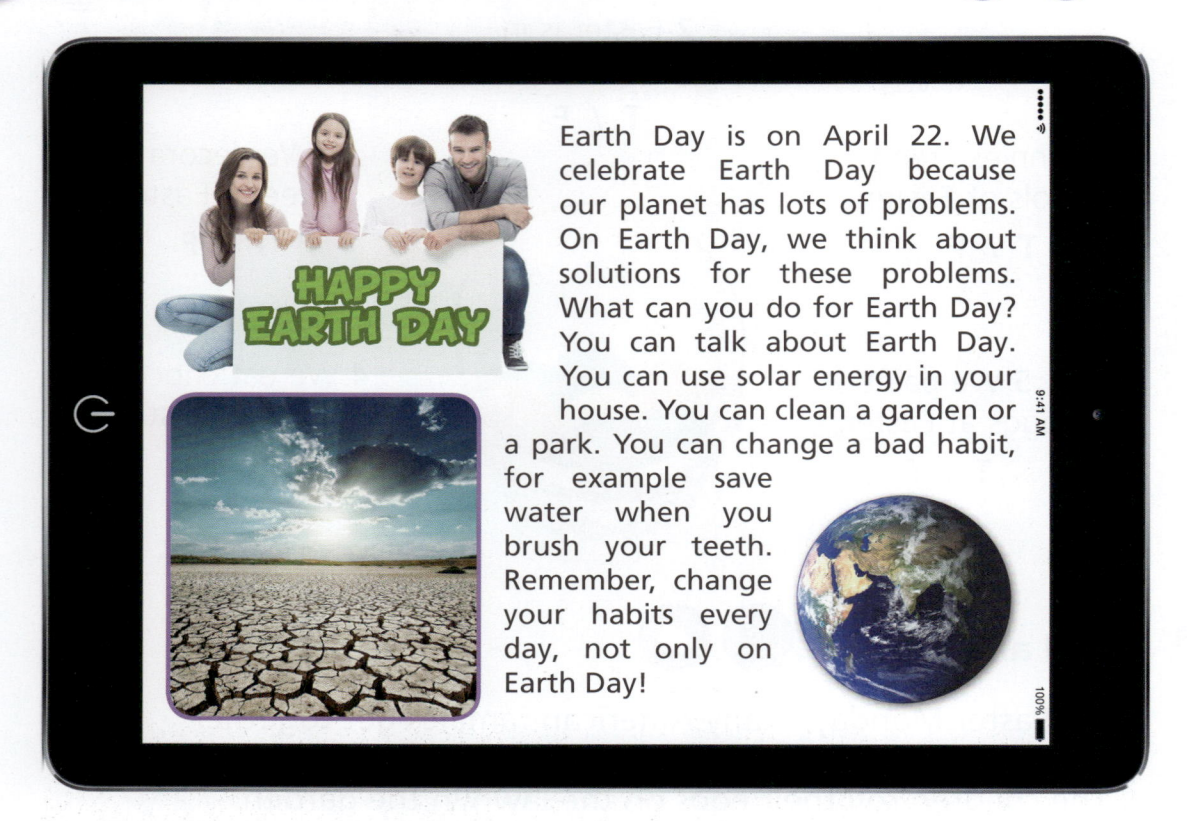

Earth Day is on April 22. We celebrate Earth Day because our planet has lots of problems. On Earth Day, we think about solutions for these problems. What can you do for Earth Day? You can talk about Earth Day. You can use solar energy in your house. You can clean a garden or a park. You can change a bad habit, for example save water when you brush your teeth. Remember, change your habits every day, not only on Earth Day!

1 Earth Day is on April 22.   T / F
2 We celebrate the things we like about Earth.   T / F
3 Only children talk about Earth Day.   T / F
4 We need Earth Day to think about our problems.   T / F
5 Families can't help on Earth Day.   T / F
6 Saving water is a bad habit.   T / F

2 Write three things you can do every day to help Planet Earth.

I can...

I can...

I can...

Earth Day

NEW English Adventure

Workbook
LEVEL 5

Contents	page
Hello	74
1. What are you good at?	78
2. There is a place for you and me	86
3. We have math on Monday	94
4. What's the matter?	102
5. My brother is younger than me	110
6. What do meerkats eat?	118
7. When I was five…	126
8. Once upon a time…	134
Happy Birthday	142
Happy Easter	143
Earth Day	144

Hello

1 **Complete and draw.**

Hi! I'm Katy. What's your _____?

Hello! My name's _____.

2 **Unscramble and write the days of the week.**

UHSRDATY   ADAUTRSY   TESAUDY   YDUNSA

MADNOY   DWYSENAED   IARDYF

1 _Thursday_ 2 _____ 3 _____ 4 _____
5 _____ 6 _____ 7 _____

3 **Find and write.**

S	C	I	S	S	O	R	S
E	N	C	I	K	P	O	N
P	E	R	A	T	I	N	F
O	U	E	C	V	M	F	L
D	P	E	N	C	I	L	Y
P	O	R	T	G	X	Y	M
E	V	E	R	T	I	M	N
N	B	O	O	K	S	N	E
I	S	U	R	U	L	E	R

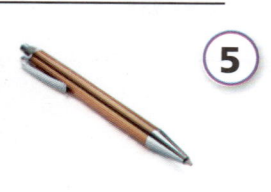

1 _sharpener_
2 _____ 
3 _____ 
4 _____
5 _____
6 _____

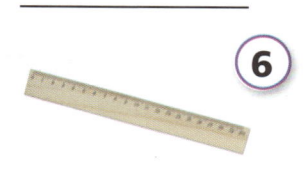

4 Unscramble the words and write questions. Match them to the answers.

1. have Do a you bike?
   Do you have a bike?

2. a have Do sister a you brother or?
   _____

3. class you 5A in Are ?
   _____

- Yes, that's right.
- Yes, I do.
- I have a brother.

5 Read and match.

1 He has a bike.
2 She has rollerblades.
3 She's in class 5B.
4 His name's Jake.

6 Complete and draw.

My friend

1 (name) This is _____.
2 (age) He's/She's _____.
3 (class) He's/She's in _____.

75

7 Look and complete the crossword puzzle.

8 Look and complete.

S__r__y.

P___a__e!

T__a__k__!

9 Use the highlighted letters to write words.

A	B	C	D	E
F	G	H	I	J
K	L	M	N	O
P	Q	R	S	T
U	V	X	Y	Z

1 __ __ __ __ __ __ __ __

2 __ __ __ __ __ __

10 Write and match.

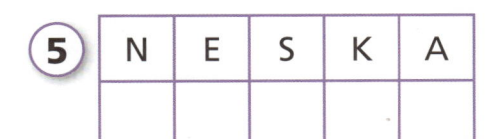

1) | O | E | O | T | R | I | S | T |
   | | | | | | | | |

2) | B | I | R | B | A | T |
   | | | | | | |

3) | R | M | H | E | T | A | S |
   | | | | | | | |

4) | H | I | S | F |
   | | | | |

5) | N | E | S | K | A |
   | | | | | |

11 Complete and stick your picture.

1 I'm in class _____.
2 I have _____.
3 I'm _____.
4 I like _____.
5 My favorite pet is _____.

Your photo

UNIT 1 What are you good at?

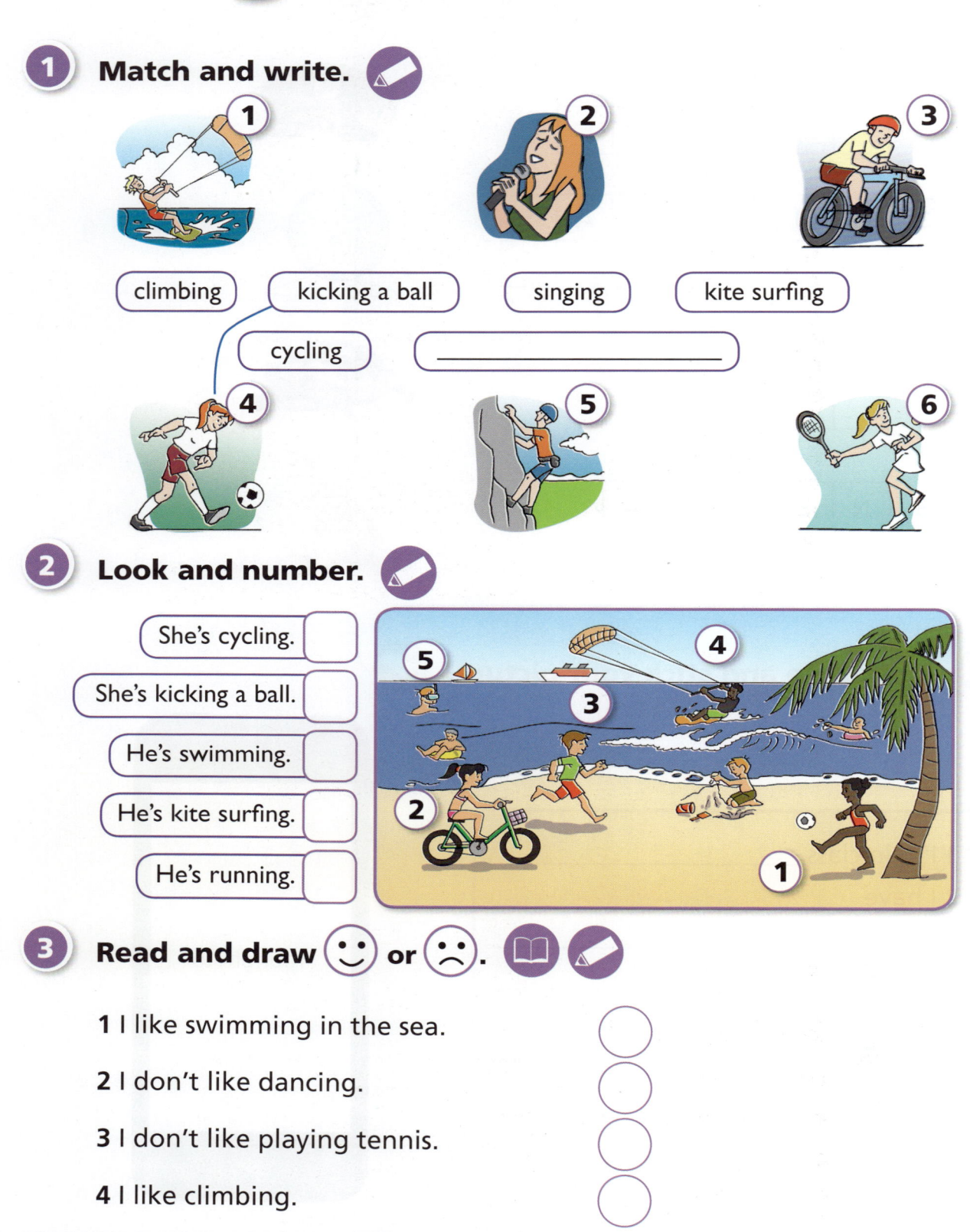

1 Match and write.

1   2   3

climbing   kicking a ball   singing   kite surfing

cycling   _____

4   5   6

2 Look and number.

She's cycling.
She's kicking a ball.
He's swimming.
He's kite surfing.
He's running.

3 Read and draw 🙂 or ☹.

1 I like swimming in the sea.
2 I don't like dancing.
3 I don't like playing tennis.
4 I like climbing.

78

4 Look and read. Then correct the sentences.

1. He's snorkeling.   No. He's kite surfing.
2. She's playing soccer.   _____
3. He's running.   _____
4. She's swimming.   _____

5 Look at the chart and write. Then write about you.

	reading	swimming	dancing	climbing	cycling
Jake	✓	✗	✗	✗	✓
Nina	✓	✓	✗	✗	✗
Steve	✗	✓	✗	✓	✓
Katy	✗	✗	✓	✓	✗
You					

1 Nina — I like reading, but I don't like climbing.

2 Steve — I like _____, but I don't like _____.

3 Jake — _____.

4 Katy — _____.

5 You — _____.

79

6 Read and write *Yes* or *No*. Then write sentences.

Do you like...?	Me
1 painting	
2 singing	
3 climbing	
4 playing tennis	

1 _____
2 _____
3 _____
4 _____

7 What are they saying? Look and write.

1. I'm good at cycling.

2.

3.

4.

8 Unscramble and write sentences.

1. you / What / doing / are

_____?

2. writing / at / good / am / I / reading / in / English

_____.

3. good / not / I'm / at / tennis / playing

_____.

4. reading, / I / don't / dancing / like / I / like / but

_____.

9 Read the chart. Check (✔) the correct answers. Then write sentences.

Are you good at...	Yes	No
1 riding a bike?		✔
2 dancing?		
3 playing volleyball?		
4 swimming?		
5 singing?		

1 *I'm not good at riding a bike.*

2 _____.

3 _____.

4 _____.

5 _____.

10 Read and complete.

| good | ~~playing~~ | running | playing | running | at |

It's Saturday morning. I'm (1) _playing_ tennis with my friend at Sportsworld. I'm (2) _____ after the ball. I can hear a voice … "Wow! You're awesome! You're really (3) _____ (4) _____ tennis!" Who is it? Well, it's Serena Wiliams. She's playing and she's (5) _____ after the ball, too! I'm (6) _____ tennis with my heroine!

11 What is your dream? Draw and write.

1 Where are you?
   _____.

2 What are you doing?
   _____
   _____
   _____.

What are you good at?

UNIT 1 EXTRA ADVENTURE

1 Circle the correct words.

1. I like playing the **violin / guitar**.
2. I **live / don't live** in a house.
3. I'm good at **singing / jumping**.
4. I **like / don't like** playing tennis.

2 Write about you. Choose activities from the chart.

playing soccer	singing	running	climbing
swimming	reading	cycling	painting
playing volleyball	kite surfing	cooking	playing tennis

1 I like _____.

2 I don't like _____.

3 I'm good at _____.

4 I'm not good at _____.

83

REVIEW 1

1 Label the activities.

playing the guitar · reading manuals
kite surfing · texting quickly
climbing · painting
cycling · fixing things

1. cycling
2. _____
3. _____
4. _____
5. _____
6. _____
7. _____
8. _____

2 Self-evaluation.

I can talk about what I'm good at and what I like.

Keep working.

Well done!

UNIT 1
OUR WORLD

1 Read and complete.

| hot-air balloon | tower | snows | the USA |

1 Niagara Falls is in Canada and in _____.

2 People visit the falls by helicopter, boat and _____.

3 There is a _____ next to the river.

4 It _____ a lot at Niagara Falls.

YOUR WORLD

1 Are there any waterfalls in your country?
   _____

2 How can you visit the waterfalls?
   _____

3 What other things can you do there?
   _____

4 Do you like visiting waterfalls?
   _____

YOUR PROJECT

Look for information about waterfalls in your country. Find photos on the Internet and make a presentation. Share it with your class.

UNIT 2 — There is a place for you and me

1 Find and circle.

(RULER) BACKPACK PENCIL ERASER SHARPENER PEN

2 Circle, unscramble and write.

This / These is my *drbasoketa* _____.
This / These are my *kboso* _____.

That / Those is my *esohu* _____.
That / Those are my *seratpn* _____.

3 Find and write. Then answer about you.

1 My grandma Louise ········· 14 Proctor Drive
2 My uncle Joe ············· 45 Ellis Road
3 My cousin Daisy ·········· 12 Elm Street
4 My aunt Mary ············· 16 Washington Square

My family lives in Turner.

1 My grandma Louise lives at _____.
2 My uncle Joe lives at _____.
3 My cousin Daisy lives at _____.
4 My aunt Mary lives at _____.

Where do you live? _____.

4 Match questions and answers.

1 Where do you live?
2 Do you like it?
3 Is there a movie theater?
4 Are there cars and trucks?

A Yes, there is a movie theater.
B I live in a big town.
C No, I don't.
D Yes, there are.

5 Name the buildings and write.

This is my town. There's a _____

_____.

6 Create a town. Complete the sign with its name. Then write about the places.

I like _____. My favorite place is _____.

There's a _____.

There are _____.

It's fabulous!

Welcome to _____!

7 Read and complete.

1. How much _____ this?
   _____ $285.

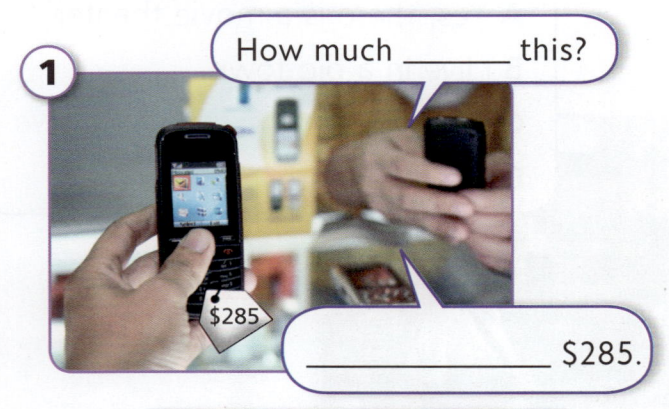

2. How much _____ these?
   _____ $57.

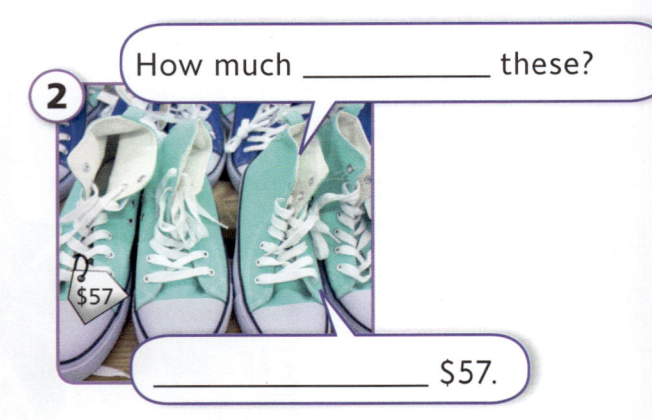

3. How _____ _____ that?
   _____ $85.

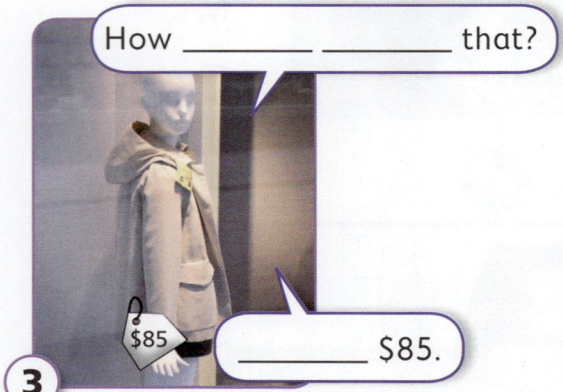

4. _____ _____ are those?
   _____'re $74.

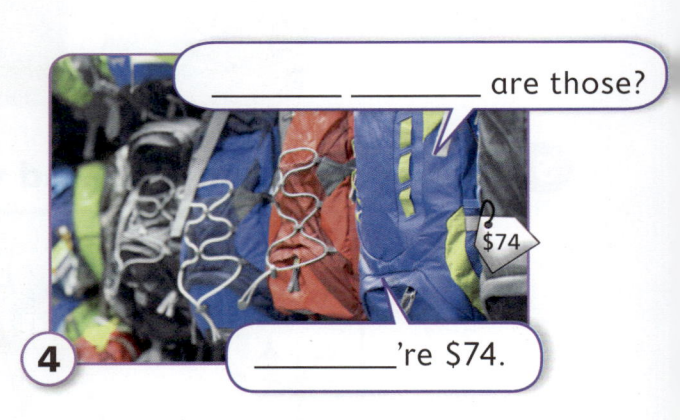

8 Read and complete with the right town. Then write about one of the other two towns.

Jacksonville    Turner    Pine Wood

There are cafés and trees. There's a drugstore. There's a beautiful square too.
It's _____.

In _____, there's a _____
_____.

9 **Look, read and number.**

○ **John:** The tree is talking to me!
○ **Pocahontas:** Where do you live, John?
   John: I live in London, England.
○ **Pocahontas:** Are there trees in London?
   John: Yes, there are, but there are lots of houses and roads, too.
○ **Pocahontas:** Is there a river in London?
   John: There's a river, but there isn't a big waterfall.
○ **Pocahontas:** This is grandmother Willow.
   John: There aren't talking trees in London!
○ **Grandmother Willow:** Hello, John Smith.
   John: What? Who's here?
○ **John:** This place is beautiful. There are trees and mountains everywhere!

10 **Read. Then use six words to complete the story.**

are	name	houses
waterfalls	beautiful	roads
talking	too	trees

Pocahontas and John are (1) _____. This is her home.
There (2) _____ mountains and (3) _____. There's a river, (4) _____! John lives in London. There are (5) _____, but there aren't waterfalls. There are lots of (6) _____ and roads.

11 **Do you remember? Write J for Julie and N for Noah.**

1. I live in the country and I love it.
2. I live in the town and it's really cool.
3. After school, my friends and I go skateboarding on the streets.
4. Every day before school I go for a walk with my dog in the mountains.

1 ☐   2 ☐

3 ☐   4 ☐

There is a place for you and me

UNIT 2 EXTRA ADVENTURE

1 Find and circle the words.

X	P	E	W	C	L	I	B	R	A	R	Y
A	I	F	E	A	I	L	C	N	E	C	P
Q	C	R	U	F	S	T	A	R	E	D	A
M	O	V	I	E	T	H	E	A	T	E	R
F	S	C	H	O	O	L	J	R	B	K	K
S	U	P	E	R	M	A	R	K	E	T	Z

2 Write the words in the correct category.

~~running~~   swimming   reading   playing soccer   snorkeling   painting

In the water   In the house   In the garden
_____   _____   _running_
_____   _____   _____

3 Circle, write the question and answer.

1. How much is (this) / these?   How much is this?
   It's 85 dollars.

2. How much are **those** / **that**?   _____

3. How much is **that** / **those**?   _____

91

REVIEW 2

1 Unscramble and write.

1. E M V O I   H T A E T R E
2. U N M T A N I S O
3. F A É C
4. L A L S A W T R E F
5. B A Y L R I R
6. V R I E S R
7. R Q A E S U
8. S E T E R
9. T U S E G O D R R
10. L D I S F E

2 What is there where you live? Write about it.

I live in _____.
There's _____.
There are _____.
In my street there's a _____.
There isn't a _____.

3 Self-evaluation.

I can talk about where I live.

Keep working.

Well done!

UNIT 2
OUR WORLD

1 Read, look and check (✓).

1 It is real.   ☐
2 It isn't real. ☐

2 Read and circle T for true and F for false.

1 A loch is a long river.	T / F
2 Loch Ness is the only loch in Scotland.	T / F
3 People like swimming in Loch Ness.	T / F
4 There are different things to do around Loch Ness.	T / F
5 Loch Ness is a very popular place for tourists.	T / F

YOUR WORLD

1 Are there lakes in your country?
_____.

2 Is the water dark?
_____.

3 Can people swim in the lakes in your country?
_____.

4 Do you like visiting lakes?
_____.

YOUR PROJECT

Look for information about lakes in your country. Find photos on the Internet and make a poster. Then present it to your class.

UNIT 3
We have math on Monday

1 Complete the crossword puzzle.

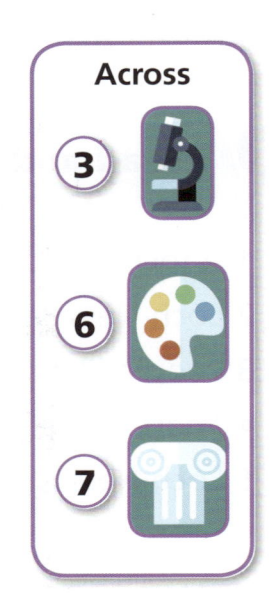

Down
1. (music)
2. (basketball)
4. (ABC)
5. (calculator)

Across
3. (microscope)
6. (palette)
7. (column)

1 Down: M U S I C

2 Read the schedule. Then complete.

Time	Monday	Tuesday	Wednesday	Thursday	Friday
9:00	English	Science	History	Math	English
11:30	Music	Geography	English	Math	English
12:30	LUNCH				
2:15	Science	English	Music	Science	Math
3:15	PE	Computer Science	Math	English	PE

In my school, we have (1) _English_ every day.
We have (2) _____ on Monday, Tuesday and Thursday,
(3) _____ only on Tuesday and (4) _____
only on Wednesday. We have (5) _____ on Monday and
Wednesday. (6) _____ science is on Tuesday, after English.
We have (7) _____ on Wednesday, Thursday and Friday.
And we have (8) _____ on Monday and Friday, at 3:15.

94

3 Look at page 23, then read. What day is it?

1. We have English in the morning and music in the afternoon. We don't have history.

   It's _____.

2. We have math and science.

   It's _____.

4 Complete.

My favorite subject is _____.

It's on _____ in the _____.

5 Read and check (✓).

	In the morning	In the afternoon
1 I play video games.		
2 I get dressed.		
3 I have breakfast.		
4 I have PE.		
5 I get up.		

6 Read and match.

1 It's twelve o'clock.

2 It's eight thirty.

3 It's five twenty.

4 It's seven thirty.

7 Look and read. Then circle T for true and F for false.

1 I wake up at six thirty.   T / F

2 I have math at eleven twenty.   T / F

3 I have lunch at twelve o'clock.   T / F

4 I have dinner at six thirty.   T / F

5 I go to bed at nine forty-five.   T / F

8 Look, read and number.

1 I wake up at five forty-five.

2 I get dressed at six ten.

3 I have breakfast at six thirty.

4 I go to school at seven fifteen.

5 I have lunch at school at twelve.

6 I go to bed at ten.

9 Match and write.

1 I get up — at 7:30. — breakfast.
2 I have — at 8:15. — to the bus stop.
3 I run — math — and art.
4 Today we have

1 <u>I get up</u>   .

2 _____.

3 _____.

4 _____.

10 Write questions. Then answer them.

- wake up
- What time
- have lunch
- have breakfast
- go to school
- do you

1. What time do you wake up? _____?
   _____.

2. _____?
   _____.

3. _____?
   _____.

4. _____?
   _____.

11 Read, draw and write.

My ideal day.

1 I get up at 🕐
_____.

2 I go to school at 🕐
_____.

3 I have lunch at 🕐
_____.

4 I do my homework at 🕐
_____.

5 I go to bed at 🕐
_____.

We have math on Monday

UNIT 3 EXTRA ADVENTURE

1 Find six school subjects. Then answer the question.

O	M	P	H	N	M	V	C	X	Z	A	H	L	H	J
U	A	C	E	N	G	L	I	S	H	E	I	K	N	D
Q	T	B	E	D	C	F	U	Y	T	A	S	P	M	S
T	H	E	N	A	O	I	V	E	A	R	T	Y	U	X
E	A	F	H	M	J	U	K	L	B	J	O	E	S	I
W	F	G	F	G	H	A	B	G	P	O	R	O	I	B
A	S	C	G	E	O	G	R	A	P	H	Y	T	C	A
C	O	M	P	U	T	E	R	S	C	I	E	N	C	E

Which two school subjects are missing?

1 _____

2 _____

2 Find and write.

1 <u>We have art at ten thirty</u>.
2 _____.
3 _____.
4 _____.

3 Write the times.

1 I get up at _____.
2 I have breakfast at _____.
3 I go to school at _____.
4 I do my homework at _____.
5 I have dinner at _____.
6 I go to bed at _____.

99

REVIEW 3

1 Find and circle.

CLASSROOMSCIENCELABRECESSARTCLASSPEMUSICPLAYGROUNDBUSSTOP

2 Read and answer.

1 What time do you get up on Monday?	
2 What time do you get up on Sunday?	
3 Do you have breakfast?	Yes No
4 Do you go to school by bus?	Yes No
5 Do you have lunch at school?	Yes No
6 What time do you do your homework?	
7 What time do you go to bed on Saturday?	

3 Self-evaluation.

I can tell the time.
I can talk about my daily routine.
I can talk about my school subjects.

Keep working.

Well done!

UNIT 3
OUR WORLD

1 **Read and circle.**

1 Longyearbyen is between Norway and the **North / South** Pole.
2 September is **colder / warmer** than January in Longyearbyen.
3 There **are / aren't** polar bears near the school.
4 We can enjoy the polar night in **winter / summer**.
5 In the summer, we can enjoy the polar **night / day**.

YOUR WORLD

1 It's summer in your town. Can you see the sun late at night?
   _____

2 It's winter in your town. Can you see the sun in the daytime?
   _____

3 Is your city warmer or colder than Longyearbyen?
   _____

4 What do you wear to school in winter?
   _____

YOUR PROJECT

Where can you find weather forecasts for your city / country? With a partner, make a list of 4 weather websites or smartphone applications. How can you share them?

UNIT 4 What's the matter?

1 Unscramble and write.

1 See / the / go / and / nurse / home.
   _____.

2 matter? / What's / the
   _____.

3 very / I / well. / feel / don't
   _____.

4 have / Do / a / toothache? / you
   _____.

2 Label the picture with the parts of the body.

arm
leg
hand
fingers
hair
feet
head

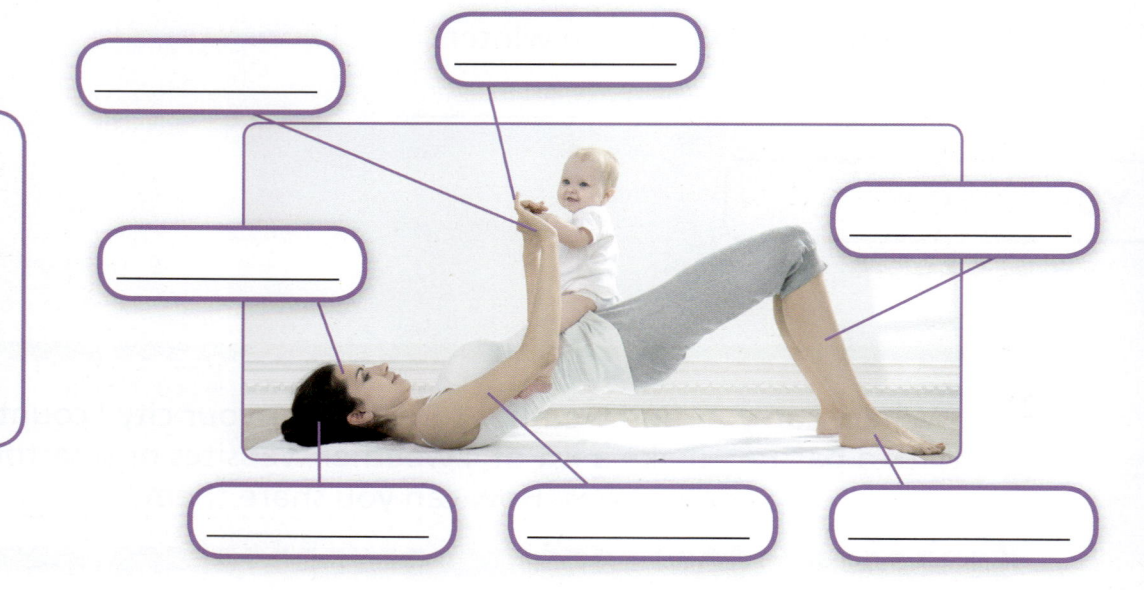

102

3 Match.

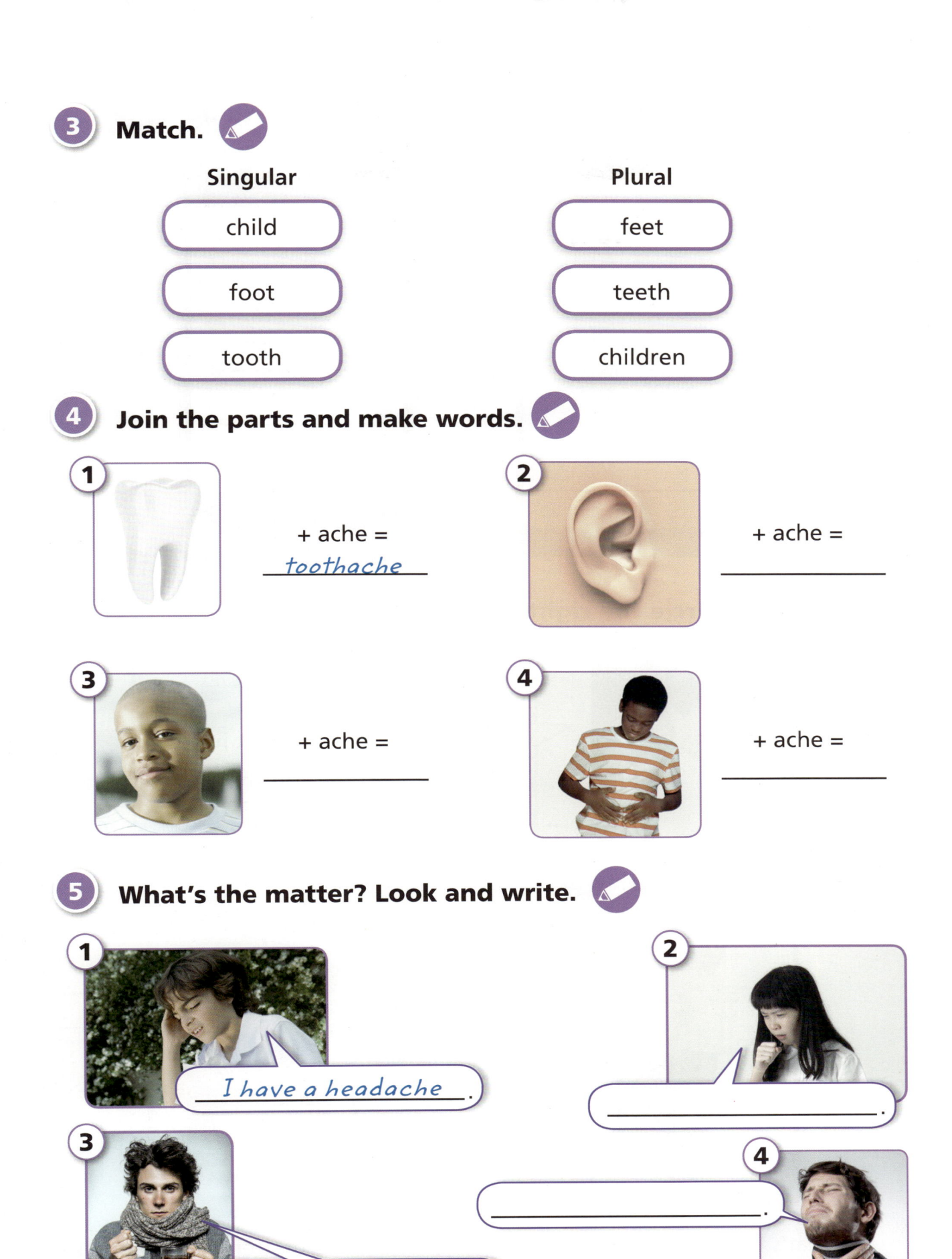

Singular
- child
- foot
- tooth

Plural
- feet
- teeth
- children

4 Join the parts and make words.

1. [tooth] + ache = _toothache_

2. [ear] + ache = _____

3. [head] + ache = _____

4. [stomach] + ache = _____

5 What's the matter? Look and write.

1. _I have a headache_.

2. _____.

3. _____.

4. _____.

6 Your friend has a cold. Write tips about what to do.

Put honey in a hot lemon drink.
_____
_____

_____
_____

7 Read and circle the right thing to do.

When I'm sick,
I eat **candy / oranges**.
I have **a soft drink / fruit juice**.
I go to **the swimming pool / bed**.
I play in **the rain / my room**.

8 Look and answer.

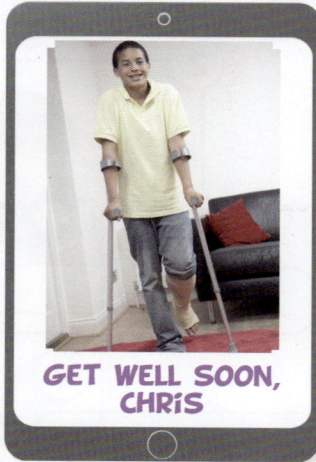

GET WELL SOON, CHRIS

GET WELL SOON, GRANDMA

1 What's the matter with Chris?
_____

2 What's the matter with Grandma?
_____

9 Match the puzzle pieces to make sentences.

- Bo Peep
- He
- Rex
- Rex has
- Now Mr. Potato Head has

- a headache.
- has an idea.
- roars.
- has a sore throat.
- a glass of water.

10 Tell the story. Write the sentences in Activity 9 in the correct order.

1 Rex has a sore throat.
2 _____
3 _____
4 _____
5 _____

11 Write the words and find the message.

1. N R D I K
2. A W E E T
3. Y E V R E
4. A Y D

_____ _____ _____ _____ .

105

12 Unscramble the words and write sentences.

I'm feeling blue. What can I do?

play let's together videogames
Let's play videogames together!

exercise! Let's some do
_____

movie! Watch a
_____.

chocolate! Eat some
_____

13 Find and circle.

C	L	E	M	O	N	R	R
N	U	R	S	E	K	W	Y
D	O	P	B	E	D	S	H
W	R	E	C	O	R	F	O
A	A	E	A	A	E	R	N
T	N	P	L	S	L	I	E
E	G	P	A	A	A	E	Y
R	E	L	P	K	X	S	A
E	X	E	R	C	I	S	E

- ~~lemon~~
- exercise
- orange
- water
- honey
- bed
- nurse
- relax

14 What are they saying? Complete.

1. Have a banana.
2. Have an _____.
3. _____.

106

UNIT 4
EXTRA ADVENTURE

What's the matter?

1 What's the matter with Jake? Read and check (✓).

Doctor: OK. How are you feeling?
Jake: Not good!
Doctor: So, you have a broken leg and a broken nose.
Jake: Ouch! And I have a bad headache and stomachache.
Doctor: Okay, Jake. Now …

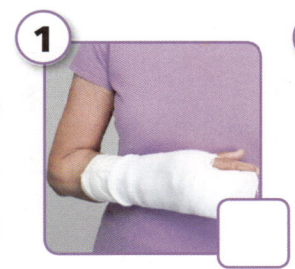

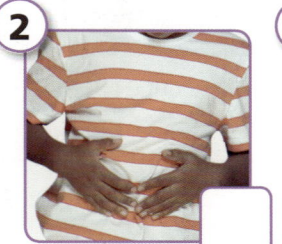

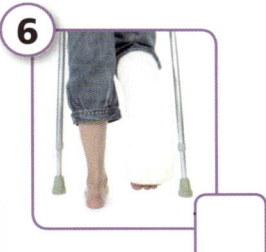

2 Complete.

Medical Report
1 _a broken leg_   2 _____   3 _____   4 _____

3 What are they saying? Circle and write.

eat your bread!

bread / fish

_____

salad / ice cream

107

REVIEW 4

1 Look at the pictures. Rewrite the sentences.

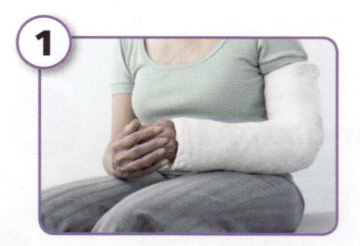

1. She has a broken leg.
_____

2. She has a stomachache.
_____

3. She has a headache.
_____

4. She has a sore throat.
_____

2 Match.

1 Eat   lots of water.
2 Drink   exercise.
3 Have   a healthy breakfast.
4 Do   an apple every day.
5 Go to   bed early.

3 Self-evaluation.

I can talk about healthy food.
I can ask and answer questions about health.

Keep working.

Well done!

UNIT 4

OUR WORLD

1 Read and number.

1 forest   2 bridge   3 river   4 waterfall

2 Do you remember? Read and circle T for true and F for false.

1 It's always sunny in Sohra.   T / F
2 There are tall, strong trees in Sohra.   T / F
3 The people of Sohra make bridges to cross rivers.   T / F
4 They cut trees to make bridges.   T / F

YOUR WORLD

1 Is it always rainy in your town?
   _____

2 Do you like rainy days?
   _____

3 Do you eat anything special on rainy days?
   _____

4 Do you play anything special on rainy days?
   _____

YOUR PROJECT

Rainy weather can be good and bad. Make a list of examples. Find photos on the Internet and make a presentation. Share it with the class.

UNIT 5 — My brother is younger than me

1 Read and complete.

> brother   older   taller   sister

1 Jake has a _____, but he doesn't have a _____.
2 Jake is _____ than his brother.
3 Jake's brother is _____ than him.
4 My brother/sister is _____ than me.

2 Find eleven months. Then answer.

F	E	B	R	U	A	R	Y
J	U	N	E	H	U	H	N
U	O	F	C	M	G	N	O
L	I	R	P	A	U	T	V
Y	A	C	V	S	S	M	E
M	P	X	E	L	T	A	M
J	A	N	U	A	R	Y	B
O	C	T	O	B	E	R	E
D	E	C	E	M	B	E	R

1 Which month is missing? _____

2 Which month is backwards? _____

3 Answer the questions.

1 Which months are long? _____

2 Which months are short? _____

3 Which months are colder? _____

4 Which months are warmer? _____

5 When's your birthday? _____

4 Use the words to describe the pictures.

> dark-haired   ~~tall~~   slim   fair-haired   short   chubby

1 __tall__
2 _____
3 _____
4 _____
5 _____
6 _____

5 Find and match the opposites. Write the missing words.

> young   chubby   dark-haired   small

1. fair-haired
2. slim
3. old
4. big

6 Look, find and write.

> bigger   chubbier   longer   shorter   smaller

This is Benny. Meet his five cousins.

Bill's ears are _____ than Benny's.

Joe's neck is _____ than Benny's.

Todd is _____ than Benny.

Fergus's nose is _____ than Benny's.

Jim's tail is _____ than Benny's.

7 Complete the chart. Then write sentences using your own ideas.

Adjective	Comparative	Adjective	Comparative
big	bigger	short	
young		small	
fast		chubby	
old		tall	

1 _____ is _____ than _____.
2 _____ is _____ than _____.
3 _____ are _____ than _____.
4 _____ are _____ than _____.

8 Look and complete.

> bigger   smaller   longer   shorter

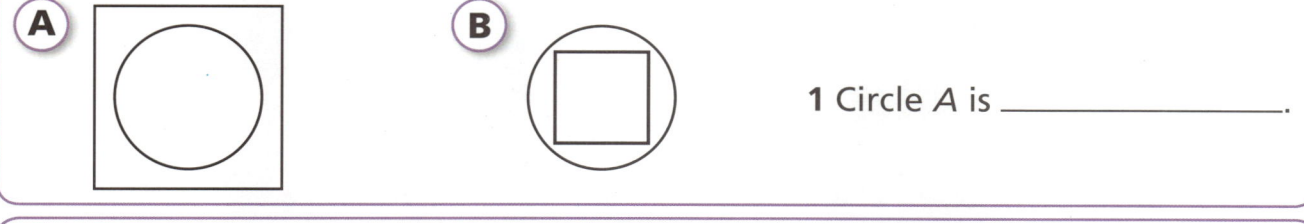

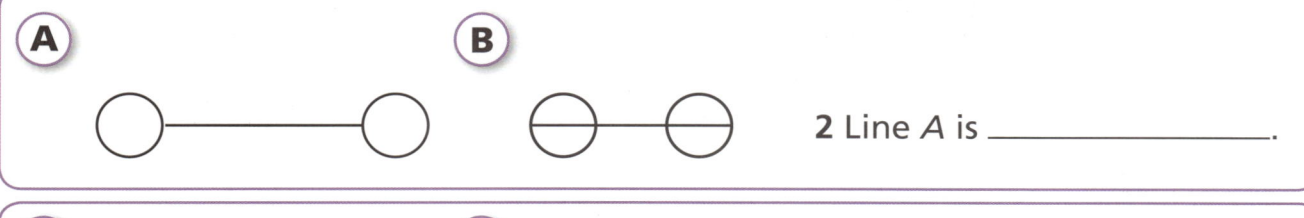

A B   1 Circle A is _____.

A B   2 Line A is _____.

A B   3 The white square in A is _____.

9 Look and write true and false sentences.

Bill   Bob   Ben

True	False
Ben is shorter than Bill.	Ben is taller than Bob.

113

10 Find the differences. Write about picture A. Use the words in the box.

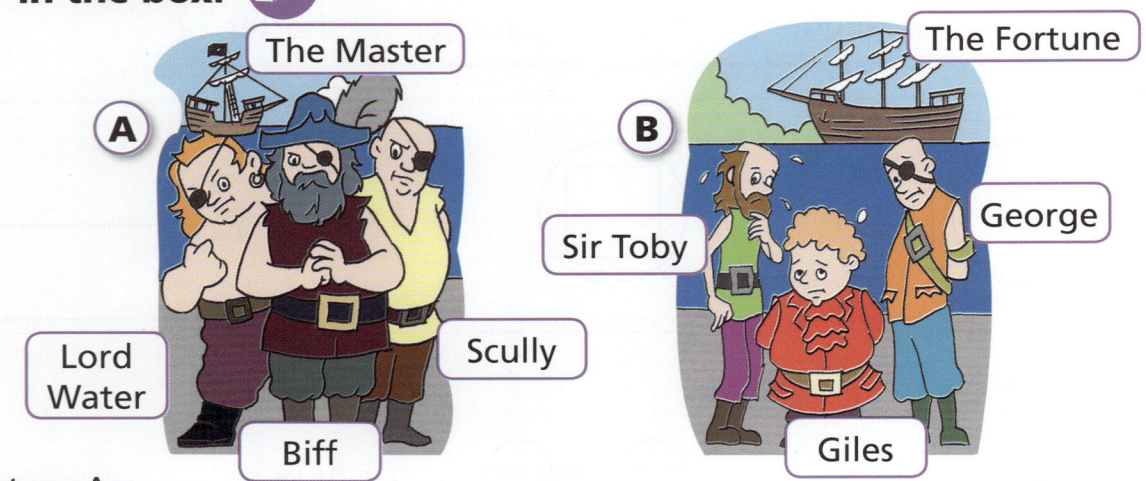

In picture A:

1 Lord Water is _____ than Sir Toby.

2 The Master is _____ than the Fortune.

3 Biff and Scully are _____ than Giles and George.

4 Giles is _____ than Biff.

5 The Fortune is _____ than The Master.

smaller
chubbier
taller
bigger
shorter

11 Write four sentences about picture B.

1 _____.

2 _____.

3 _____.

4 _____.

12 Read and answer *Yes* or *No*.

1 Are you taller than your teacher? _____.

2 Are you older than Jake? _____.

3 Is Katy smaller than you? _____.

4 Is Nina younger than you? _____.

My brother is younger than me

UNIT 5 EXTRA ADVENTURE

1 Compare and write.

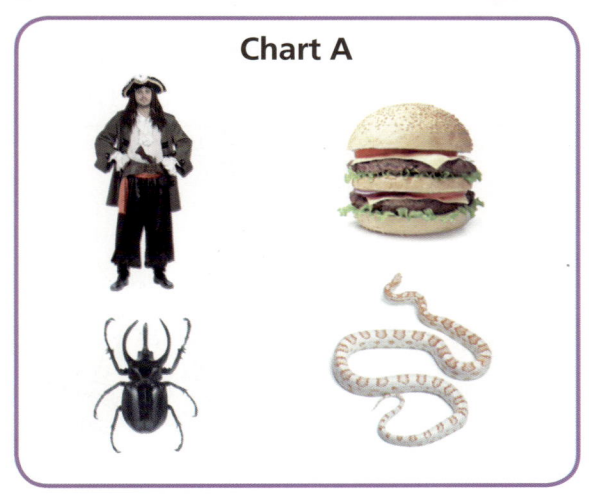

Chart A

Chart B

In chart A:

1 *The pirate is younger.*
2 _____
3 _____
4 _____

2 Are these sentences true about you? Rewrite the false ones.

1 I'm taller than my best friend.   T / F
_____

2 I'm shorter than my teacher.   T / F
_____

3 I'm younger than my neighbor.   T / F
_____

115

REVIEW 5

1 Write about the opposites.

1. A big mouse with a long tail.
2. A slim rabbit with short ears. 
3. A tall girl. She is dark-haired.
4. An old man with short hair.

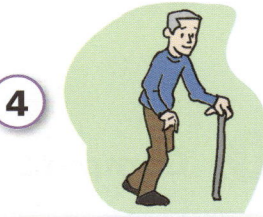

1. A small mouse with a short tail.
2. _____
3. _____
4. _____

2 Look and read. Then circle T for true and F for false.

1 Lester has bigger ears than Larry.   T / F
2 Larry has longer ears than Lester.   T / F
3 Lester is chubbier than Larry.   T / F
4 Larry is darker than Lester.   T / F

3 Self-evaluation.

I can describe and compare people and things.
I can say the months of the year.

Keep working.

Well done!

UNIT 5 OUR WORLD

1 Look, read and match.

A   B   C

1 The people are resting in an oasis. ◯

2 The picture is in a cave. ◯

3 The Sahara is very dry and very windy. ◯

2 Read, find and cross out the wrong information.

1 The desert is hot, ~~rainy~~ and windy.

2 There aren't fields, waterfalls or an oasis in the Sahara desert.

3 The Sahara was rainy, green and cold 5000 years ago.

4 The ancient paintings show men swimming, giraffes and elephants.

YOUR WORLD

1 Is there a desert in your country?
_____

2 Are there forests in your country?
_____

YOUR PROJECT

> Identify four more deserts that were forests in ancient times. Find information about them on the Internet. Make a list and share it with the class.

UNIT 6 What do meerkats eat?

1 Look and write.

1. _giant panda_
2. _____
3. _____
4. _____
5. _____
6. _____

2 Match the pieces. Then write the names of the bears.

| Polar bear | Brown bear | Giant panda |

1. Their fur is — the Arctic. — 1 _____
2. They live in — meat and plants. — 2 _____
3. They eat — black and white. — 3 _____

118

3 Circle the correct word to complete the sentences.

Polar bears live in **the Arctic Circle / Antarctica**. They live **in the sea / on trees**. They sleep **during the day / at night**. They eat **fruits and vegetables / meat** from animals like seals.

4 Find one mistake in each sentence. Then rewrite it.

1 Chimpanzees live in Europe. Their fur is dark. Their favorite food is bananas.
_____

2 Bison are small animals. They live in forests. They eat grass and plants.
_____

3 Giant Pandas live in China. They eat meat. They sleep under trees.
_____

5 Look and complete.

1 bats   2 foxes   3 birds

1 Where do _____ sleep? They sleep in nests.

2 Where do _____ sleep? They sleep in caves.

3 Where do _____ sleep? They sleep in dens.

6 Find, circle and classify.

RABBIT FISH SNAKE HAMSTER ZEBRA HIPPO CAT MEERKAT CHIMPANZEE

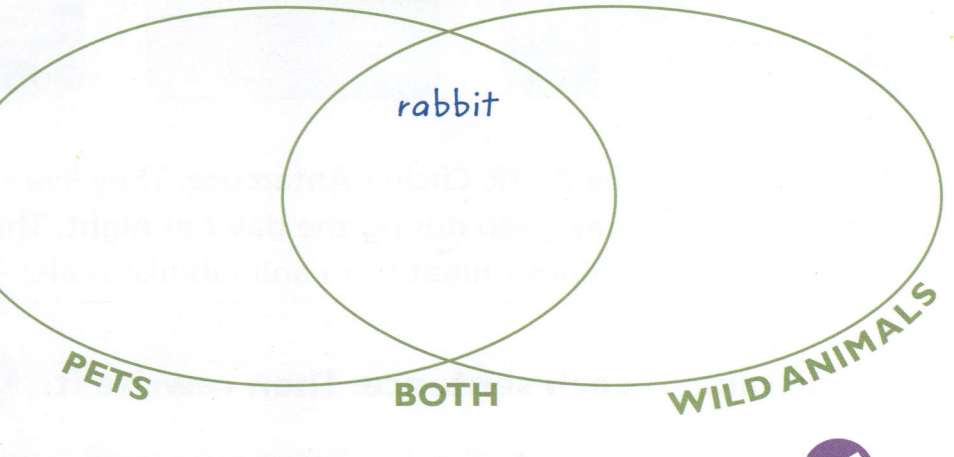

rabbit

PETS   BOTH   WILD ANIMALS

7 Look and check (✓). Then write the answers.

	fish	seeds	vegetables
Luke and Bella			
Phyllis and George			
Romeo and Juliet			

1 What do Luke and Bella eat? They eat _____.

2 What do Phyllis and George eat? They _____.

3 What do Romeo and Juliet eat? _____.

8 Read and write four true sentences.

| Grasshoppers Ants | can are have | swim / fly / jump big / strong / small fur / wings / legs |

1 _____ .
2 _____ .
3 _____ .
4 _____ .

9 Unscramble and write.

1 l f y

2 e b e

3 e t b e l e

_____   _____   _____

10 Which bugs are these? Read and write.

1 They're bigger than flies. They're black and yellow. _____

2 They're smaller than beetles. They are black. _____

121

11 Look at the pets. Then write.

1	Lulu and Leo	(carrots)	(meat ✗)
2	Billy and Joel	(dog food)	(chocolate ✗)
3	Meg and Mog	(seeds)	(fish ✗)

1 Lulu and Leo are _rabbits_. They eat _____. They don't eat _____.
2 Billy and Joel _____. They _____. They don't _____.
3 Meg and Mog _____.

12 Read and write the message.

2-9 5-9 1-10 1-11
5-8 1-8 7-9 2-9
6-9 1-8 5-9 5-10

	1	2	3	4	5	6	7
8	A	B	C	D	E	F	G
9	H	I	J	K	L	M	N
10	O	P	Q	R	S	T	U
11	V	W	X	Y	Z	-	-

_I_ _____

13 Find six animals. Then write four sentences.

C	I	F	H	A	N
R	B	E	A	R	H
O	P	C	M	A	H
C	A	T	S	B	F
O	N	Z	T	B	I
D	D	E	E	I	S
I	A	B	R	T	H
L	B	R	J	W	G
E	I	A	P	R	O
Z	G	K	N	Y	S

eat   live   sleep

1 _Fish live in the sea._
2 _____.
3 _____.
4 _____.
5 _____.

What do meerkats eat?

UNIT 6 EXTRA ADVENTURE

1 Read, choose and circle. Then answer.

Matt: Do you have a pet?
Gemma: Yes, I do. His name's Fluffy.
Matt: Fluffy? Nice name!
Gemma: Yes. Fluffy is a mouse.
Matt: A mouse!?
Gemma: That's right. His fur is short and brown.
Matt: And what does he eat?
Gemma: He eats chicken and he likes cheese, too.
Matt: Cool! And does he sleep in your bed?
Gemma: No, he doesn't. He sleeps in a box.

My pet is a small **dog / mouse**. His fur is **short / long** and **brown / pink**. He eats **chicken / popcorn** and he likes **rice / cheese**, too. He sleeps in a **bed / box**. His name's **Fluffy / Funny**.

1 What's the pet's name?
_____.

2 What does it eat?
_____.

3 Where does it sleep?
_____.

2 Write about your pet. Answer the questions.

1 What's your pet? _____.
2 What's its name? _____.
3 What does it eat? _____.
4 Where does it sleep? _____.

REVIEW 6

1 Read, circle and draw.

1 Troy and Trudy are **dogs / crocodiles**.

2 They live in **rivers / the countryside**.

3 They are from **the UK / Africa**.

4 They sleep in **the river / a kennel**.

2 Use the words in the box to write questions. Then answer.

> What   sleep   Troy and Trudy   eat   are   live   color   Where   do

1 <u>What are Troy and Trudy</u> ? _____.
2 _____ ? _____.
3 _____ ? _____.
4 _____ ? _____.
5 _____ ? _____.

3 Self-evaluation.

I can ask and answer questions about pets and wild animals.

Keep working.

Well done!

UNIT 6
OUR WORLD

1 **Read and match.**

1 The Outback is
2 Uluru is special
3 It can be
4 Most people visit

A the central region of the Outback.
B very big.
C for Aboriginal people.
D very hot or very cold in the Outback.

YOUR WORLD

1 Are there wild animals in your country?
_____

2 It is July. What's the weather like in your country?
_____

3 It is December. What's the weather like in your country?
_____

YOUR PROJECT

Many different areas in Australia are part of the Outback. Look for information and pictures on the Internet about a different part of the Outback. Make a poster and present it to your class.

UNIT 7 When I was five...

1 Find and circle. Then answer.

OLDSHORTSMALLTINYSADHUGECURLYSLIMSTRAIGHTYOUNGTALLDARKBIGFAIRCHUBBYHAPPY

There is a word that is new. It's the opposite of *huge*. What is it?
_____

2 Write the opposites.

sad — *happy*	_____ — young	_____ — huge
_____ — tall	dark — _____	straight — _____
_____ — short	big — _____	chubby — _____

3 Match.

THEN ...

1 Nick was 5 years old.
2 He was short.
3 Nick's hair was short and dark.
4 His favorite sport was soccer.

NOW

Now his hair is fair. ◯
Now it's skateboarding. ◯
Now he's tall. ◯
Now he's 13 years old. ◯

126

4 Find and write about the children when they were younger.

1 Nick .... 1 meter 10 centimeters tall at 5.
2 Katy .... 1 meter 13 centimeters tall at 5.
3 Steve .... 1 meter 5 centimeters tall at 5.
4 Nina .... 1 meter tall at 4.
5 Jake .... 1 meter 3 centimeters tall at 4.

1 Nick *was 1 meter 5 centimeters tall at 5.*
2 Katy _____
3 Steve _____
4 Nina _____
5 Jake _____

1 Who was taller than Nick at 5? _____
2 Was Katy taller or shorter than Jake at 4? _____

5 Read. Then write *Lucy* or *Liz*.

1 When Liz was 5 years old, her hair was long and dark. She was 1 meter 5 centimeters tall. Her favorite place was the beach.

2 When Lucy was 6 years old, her hair was long and straight. She was 1 meter 12 centimeters tall. Her favorite hobby was reading.

_____   _____

127

6 **Read and match.**

1 I was 3 years old. I was at the park with my parents. The bike was new. My grandpa was happy, but I was scared.

2 I was 4 years old. I was at the beach with my parents and my brother. We were on vacation!

3 I was 2 years old. I was at the soccer field with my dad. Soccer was my favorite sport. It was fun!

4 I was 4 years old. I was with my twin brother. It was our first day at school. We were happy.

7 **Draw a picture of you when you were five. Write about it.**

I was _____
_____
_____.

8 Label the parts of the dinosaur's body.

9 Look, read and match.

1. How big was this dinosaur?
2. How long were its claws?
3. Was it a meat eater?
4. Were its teeth big?
5. Was its body long?

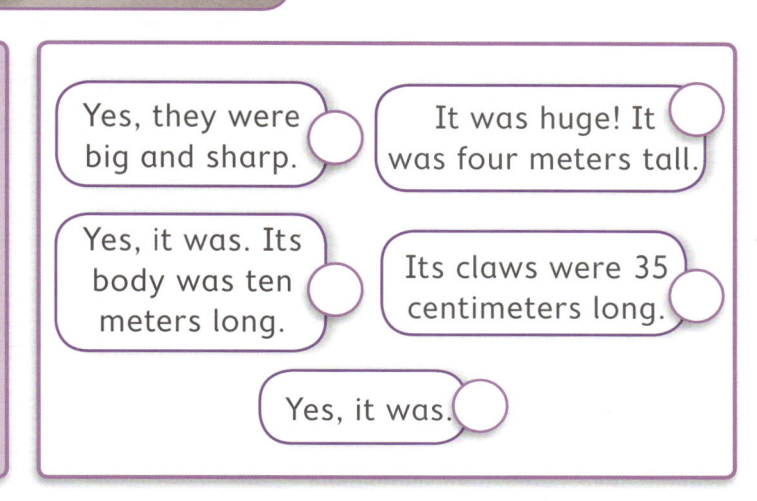

- Yes, they were big and sharp.
- It was huge! It was four meters tall.
- Yes, it was. Its body was ten meters long.
- Its claws were 35 centimeters long.
- Yes, it was.

129

10 **Read and circle T for true or F for false.**

1 Scientists have photos of dinosaurs.   T / F
2 Scientists study dinosaurs.   T / F
3 They study animal fossils.   T / F

11 **Read and check (✓) the correct picture.**

This is a Stegosaurus. Its tail was short and its neck was short too. Its body was big, but its head was small. Its back was full of sharp spikes.

12 **Look at the other dinosaur in Activity 11. Write four sentences about it.**

1 Its neck was long.
2 _____.
3 _____.
4 _____.

13 **Classify the words.**

body   claws   head   strong   huge   long
neck   sharp   short   spikes   teeth   tiny

Parts of a dinosaur	Adjectives
body	

When I was five...

UNIT 7 EXTRA ADVENTURE

1 Do the memory quiz.

http://www.englishadventure.com.br

ENGLISH ADVENTURE

DO THE QUICK MEMORY QUIZ – Look at the images. Write *(T) True* or *(F) False*. Get 2 Adventure points for each correct answer.

Unit Hello and 1

Katy doesn't like playing tennis.

Unit 2

Steve lives at 12 Exeter Drive, in Turner.

Unit 3

Nina gets up at 8:15.

Unit 4

Jake has a cold.

Unit 5

Jake is older than his brother.

Unit 6

Brown bears sleep in cages.

Unit 7

Nina's hair was short.

Quiz results:

13 - 14 Adventure Points – Well done! Your memory is excellent!

09 - 11 Adventure Points – You have very good memory. Well done!

5 - 7 Adventure Points – Your memory is good.

1 - 3 Adventure Points – Well, what do you think?

REVIEW 7

1 Write *was* or *were*. Check (✓) the right picture.

The monster (1) _was_ in the forest. Its body (2) _____ strong, but its head (3) _____ small. Its legs (4) _____ strong and its tail (5) _____ very long. Its teeth (6) _____ very sharp. Its ears (7) _____ small, but its nose (8) _____ big.

2 Write about yourself.

1 When I was _____, my hair was _____.
2 When I was _____, my toys were _____.
3 When I was _____, my best friend _____.
4 When I was _____, my hobby _____.

3 Self-evaluation.

I can talk about the past.
I can talk about dinosaurs.

Keep working.

Well done!

UNIT 7 OUR WORLD

1 Read and circle.

1 Kiribati has many **small / big** islands.
2 There **is / isn't** a lot of space.
3 The sea is **low / high**.
4 People build **bridges / walls** from rocks.

YOUR WORLD

Think about where you live and answer the questions.

1 Is anything different now?
_____

2 Are there any islands in the area where you live?
_____

YOUR PROJECT

Are there other islands like Kiribati? Look for information about islands on the Internet. Make a poster and present it to your class.

UNIT 8 Once upon a time...

1 Look at page 63, read and complete.

1 The name of the kingdom was **Idyllia / Roderick**.
2 There was a scary **dragon / knight** in the kingdom.
3 The people in the kingdom were **happy / scared**.
4 Phillip was old and **scared / young** and clever.
5 The dragon **was / wasn't** happy with the church bells.
6 At the end of the play, the people in the kingdom were **free and happy / scared and sad**.

2 Look, read and answer.

Philip

The dragon

1 Was Philip brave? _Yes, he was._
2 Was Philip evil?
No, _____. _____ good.
3 Was the dragon good?
_____. It was very bad.
4 Was the dragon scary?
_____.
5 Was Philip clever?
_____.

3 Complete the invitation.

INVITATION

_____ School Theater Group
(school name)

Showing: _____
(name of the play)

When? _____

What time? _____

4 What kind of book is it? Look and match.

e.t. invasion **1**
Summer of love **2**
THE LIFE OF JULIUS CESAR **3**
THE MYSTERY OF WIZARD'S HALL **4**
AROUND THE WORLD WITH FINN **5**

Adventure ○
History ○
Magic and wizards ○

Romance ○
Science fiction ○

5 Match and write.

Hercules — Greece
Robin Hood   Egypt
Pocahontas   the United States
Cleopatra   the United Kingdom

1 <u>Hercules was from Greece</u>.
2 _____.
3 _____.
4 _____.

6 Change the words. Write about Philip, the hero in the story on page 63.

> Hercules was from Greece. He was a famous hero. He was very strong.

1 Philip was _____.
2 He was _____.
3 He _____.

135

7 Complete the chart with the words from the word cloud. Then add more words.

Word cloud: listening to music, running, clever, science fiction, strong, history, fantasy, brave, playing tennis, romance

characteristics	likes and dislikes	types of book

8 Use the words from Activity 7 to write sentences.

1 Matt
1 Matt likes running.
2 He is brave.
3 He reads history books.

2 Olivia
1 _____.
2 _____.
3 _____.

3 Rachel and Fred
1 _____.
2 _____.
3 _____.

9 Look, read and write the number to put the story in the correct order. 📖 ✏️

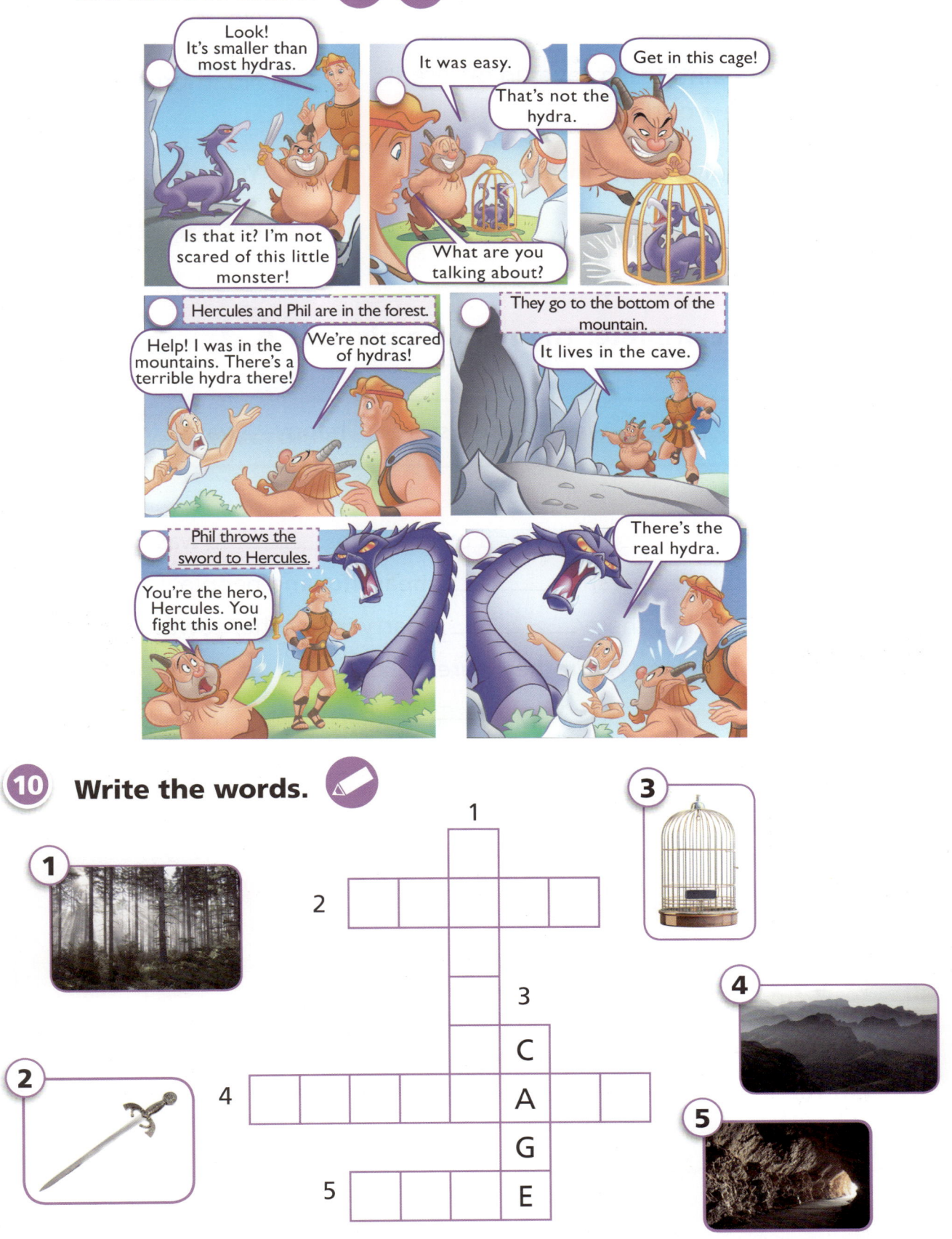

10 Write the words. ✏️

11 Read and match.

1 Were there books a long time ago?

2 Are there paintings in caves in different parts of the world?

3 Are there only people in the paintings?

4 Who were the artists?

◯ No, there aren't.

◯ No, there weren't.

◯ Yes, there are.

◯ It is a mystery.

12 Read and complete. Then draw a picture.

> time   name   was   were   scared   happy   wasn't

Once upon a _____ there was a queen. Her _____ was Penelope. She was very brave, but she _____ beautiful and people _____ scared of her. One day, there _____ a party in another town. There were lots of people at the party, but they weren't _____ of Penelope. She was very _____.

Once upon a time...

UNIT 8 EXTRA ADVENTURE

1 Answer the questions.

1 Where do you live?
_____

2 What do you like to read?
_____

3 What are you good at?
_____

4 What can you do?
_____

2 Complete the chart about you.

1 Favorite book genre:	
2 Book title:	
3 Theme of its story:	
4 Main character:	
5 His/Her characteristics:	
6 Thing(s) he/she is good at:	
7 Thing(s) he/she can do:	

3 Use the information in Activity 2 to complete the text. Circle *He* or *She*.

I like (1) _____ books. My favorite book is (2) _____.
It is about (3) _____ . (4) _____ is the main character.
He / She is (5) _____ . He / She is good at
(6) _____ He / She can (7) _____.

139

REVIEW 8

1 Find the words.

mountain ~~mountain~~

P	M	O	U	N	T	A	I	N	S	R	T	I	M
U	E	C	L	G	M	G	F	F	Y	X	E	Q	K
D	C	S	U	P	E	R	M	A	R	K	E	T	O
F	A	A	C	O	V	N	H	O	B	S	S	S	M
P	O	I	S	U	H	A	B	F	G	D	K	Q	C
K	R	R	C	T	T	T	L	C	L	S	T	U	M
U	P	W	E	M	L	V	N	E	U	N	Q	A	J
X	I	D	Y	S	E	E	I	I	S	C	E	R	N
S	T	X	C	H	T	F	B	R	L	D	A	E	H
U	Z	A	X	K	C	H	U	R	C	H	J	U	H

church

supermarket

castle

square

forest

fields

2 Read and write the correct words.

> can   doesn't   good at   has   is   likes   lives

My super hero's name _____ Red Man. He _____ in New York. He _____ X-ray vision and _____ fly. He _____ running, but he _____ like swimming. He is _____ protecting people from crime.

3 Self-evaluation.

> I can talk about heroes from the past.
> I can understand and enjoy stories.
> I can say what kind of reading I like.

Keep working.

Well done!

140

UNIT 8 OUR WORLD

1 Read and answer.

1 Is Antarctica a desert?

_____.

2 Does it rain a lot in Antarctica?

_____.

3 Which continent is Antarctica bigger than?

_____.

4 What animals are there in Antarctica?

_____.

YOUR WORLD

Imagine you are going to Antarctica. Check THREE things to take with you. Why do you take them?

- Winter clothes ☐
- Tablet with 4G ☐
- Smartphone with 4G ☐
- Sunglasses ☐
- Food and water ☐
- Video games ☐
- Sneakers ☐
- Tent ☐
- Sun block ☐

Reason: _____

_____

YOUR PROJECT

Make a poster about what you need to survive in Antarctica and why. Look for information and photos on the internet. Then present your poster to your class.

HAPPY BIRTHDAY

1 Read and complete.

> birthday   eleven   candles   October   party

It's my birthday in _____ . This year I'm _____. I always have a birthday _____ with all of my friends and family. I love eating _____ cake, especially chocolate cake! There are eleven _____ on my cake.

2 Unscramble and write the questions.

1 is / birthday? / When /your
_____.

2 is / time / What / party? / the
_____.

3 inviting? / Who / you / are
_____.

4 your / How / are / on / cake? / many / candles / there
_____.

3 Draw an invitation for your birthday party. Then answer the questions from Activity 2.

1 _____.
2 _____.
3 _____.
4 _____.

142

HAPPY EASTER

1 Read and match.

1 On Easter Day, we can find

2 Sometimes Easter in March

3 A symbol of Easter is

4 The Easter Egg Roll is

5 We can paint Easter eggs

A a tradition in the USA.

B chocolate eggs in the garden.

C in different colors.

D and sometimes it is in April.

E a bunny.

2 Unscramble the words and write. Then read and match the correct basket.

The eggs in my (abkets) _____ are big. They are many (rtfdifene) _____ colors. The blue eggs were a present from my (dgmran) _____ a and the red eggs were a present from my (ucsion) _____. There is also one (erneg) _____ egg and one brown egg.

3 Write about you.

1 On Easter Day, I eat _____.

2 My family and I _____.

3 I like/don't like Easter because _____.

EARTH DAY

1 Look and match the sentences to the pictures.

1 It's always rainy in some parts of the world.

2 It is hotter now than in the past.

3 Chemicals are bad for sea animals.

4 The weather can destroy towns.

2 Are these problems or solutions? Write in the correct column.

recycle   use solar energy   use plastic cups   go by car
take a long shower   turn off the light   use plastic bags   save water

Problems	Solutions

3 What does Jake do to help Planet Earth? Unscramble and write.

1 take / I / don't / long / shower. / a
   _____.

2 to / I / school. / walk
   _____.

3 the / computer. / off / I / turn
   _____.

4 local / I / the / park. / clean
   _____.

I help the planet!

The publisher would like to thank the following for their kind permission to reproduce their photographs:

(Key: photos are lettered from L-R on the page)

2a: Tiler84/iStockphotos; 2b: Boschettophotography/iStockphotos; 2c: StockPhotosArt/iStockphotos; 2d: NY59/iStockphotos; 2e Gelpi/iStockphotos; 2f Picsfive/iStockphotos; 2g Vicm/iStockphotos; 2h Kreativebrain/iStockphotos; 3a Mertsalov_Andrii/Thinkstock; 3b bike3c roller blades 3d Hill Street Studios/Thinkstock; 3e Leontura/Thinkstock; 4a peanut8481/Thinkstock; 4b Jupiterimages/Thinkstock; 4c Wavebreakmedia Ltd/Thinkstock; d stray_cat/istock; 5a jantroyka/Thinkstock; 5b Studioimagen/iStockphotos; 5c GlobalP/iStockphotos; 5d GlobalP/iStockphotos; 5eAluxum/iStockphotos; 5f ABV/iStockphotos; 5g Futureimage/iStockphotos; 5h Tempusfugit/iStockphotos; 5i Tanuha2001/iStockphotos; 5j Lightkeeper/iStockphotos ; 5k Ene/iStockphotos passaro; 5m GlobalP/iStockphotos; 5l © Erba78 | Dreamstime.com; 7 shalamov/Thinkstock; 9 Kary Nieuwenhuis/Thinkstock; 11a videnovic/Thinkstock; 11b Brand X Pictures/Thinkstock; 11c Top PhotoCorporation/Thinkstock; 11d prudkov/Thinkstock; 12a menino gbh007/Thinkstock; 12b; gbh007/Thinkstock; 13a Bloomberg/Contributor; 13b © Chiyacat | Dreamstime.com; 16 WavebreakmediaLtd/Thinkstock; 17a Ingram Publishing/Thinkstock; 17b Vectomart/Thinkstock; 17c Zoonar/P.Malyshev/Thinkstock; 17d Pogonici/Thinkstock; 19a Jupiterimages/Thinkstock; 19b Purestock/Thinkstock; 19c Luoman/iStockphotos; 21a ©Petr Švec; 21b © Bo Li|Dreamstime; 21c Osorioartist | Dreamstime.com; 25a Rawpixel Ltd/Thinkstock; 25b Anastasiia_M/Thinkstock; 25c DragonImages/Thinkstock; 25d Auimeesri/Thinkstock; 25e menino com pipoca Subodhsathe/Thinkstock; 25f Robert Wilson/Thinkstock; 25g video game Merznatalia/Thinkstock; 27b Wavebreakmedia Ltd/Thinkstock; 27a menino Gepi/Shutterstock; 28a onibus Robert Wilson/Thinkstock; 28b joxxxxjo/Thinkstock; 28c Thinkstock; 28d GlobalP/Thinkstock; 28e pioneer111/Thinkstock; 28f neskez/Thinkstock; 28g Alto Contraste SP; 28h MattKay/Thinkstock; 28i instrumentos musicais orlov345/Thinkstock; 28j criancas conversando 29a/c ©TylerOlson|Dreamstime.com; 29b ©AleksandrLutcenko|Dreamstime.com; 32a/b/c/d/e/g/j Dreams/iStock; 32h Bolgna/iStockphotos; 32i ©Es75|Dreamstime.com; 32k JacekChabraszewski/iStockphotos; 32l anna1311/iStockphotos; 32m Jupiterimages/Thinkstock; 33a Paul Moore/Thinkstoc; 33b AndreyPopov/Thinkstock; 33c AndreyPopov/Thinkstock; 33d JPC-PROD/Thinkstock; 33e Tom Le Goff/Thinkstock; 33f kicsiicsi/Thinstock; 35a leungchopan/Thinkstock; 35b vystek-photographie/iStockphotos; 36a fotofreaks/Thinkstock; 36b vadimguzhva/Thinkstock; 36cka2shka/Thinkstock; 36d Tom Le Goff/Thinkstock; 36f tinnapong/Thinkstock; 36eiStock; 37a © Buddha13|Dreamstime.com; 37b Danielrao/iStock Photo; 40a abstractdesignlabs/Thinkstock; 40b/c WavebreakmediaLtd/Thinkstock; 40c ChristopherRobbins/Thinkstock; 40d monkeybusinessimages/Thinkstock; 40e Pixland/Thinkstock; 43a Fuse/ThinkStock; 43b duas nenes gemeas 43c Jeff Wheeler/TNS/ZUMA PRESS/Glow Images; 43d Imagecollect/Dreamstime.com; 44a SolStock/Thinkstock; 44b Jack Hollingsworth/Thinkstock; 44c Mike Watson Images/Thinkstock; 44d m-imagephotography/Thinkstock; 44e Jani Bryson 45a ©Wrangel | Dreamstime.com; 45b Jason Edwards/Getty Images; 47a Nazzu/iStockphotos; 47d tiero/iStockphotos; 47g Urban WaldenstrAm/iStockphotos; 47b sementes lindavostrovska/Thinkstock, 47f grama, 44e karandaev/Thinkstock; 48a ©Hupeng|Dreamstime.com; 48bFlinster007/Thinkstock; 48c oksanaphoto/Thinkstock; 48davebreakmedia Ltd/Thinkstock; 49a©Nikolai Tsvetkov | Dreamstime.com; 49b JackF/Thinkstock; 49c IgorKovalchuk/Thinkstock; 49d iStock; 49e Nneirda/Thinkstock; 49fiStock; 51d Comstock/Thinkstock; 51e MarcusMacksad/Thinkstock; 51f zilli/iStockphotos; 51c © Isselee | Dreamstime.com; 51b Nengloveyou | Dreamstime.com; 51a VladimirFLloyd/Thinkstock; 52a © Elwynn | Dreamstime.com; 52b © Monkey Business Images | Dreamstime.com; 52c mediaphotos/iStockphotos; 53a dreams time ID 533252; 53b 1518282; 55a/b Brian McEntire/Thinkstock; 56 Stockbyte/Thinkstock; 59a Dorling Kindersley/Thinkstock; 59b fossil KatarzynaBialasiewicz/Thinkstock; 59c ©Mr1805 | Dreamstime.com; 53d janscherders/Thinkstock; 60a© Freerlaw | Dreamstime.com; 60b para827/Thinkstock; 61a © Sorin Colac | Dreamstime.com; 61b ©Confidential Information | Dreamstime.com; 63 rafico2013/istock; 64a Andrea Carolina Sanchez Gonzalez/istock; 64b nikolaj2/istock; 64c Sylphe_7/istock; 64d cookelma/istock; 64e Juli_Rose/istock; 64f dolgachov/istock; 64a/b syntika/istock; 65c/d Gromit702/istock; 67a Corbis/Getty images; 67b ©Greg Epperson|Dreamstime.com; 67c ©Photowitch|Dreamstime.com; 68f Wavebreakmedia/Thinkstock; 68a StefanieDegner/Thinkstock; 68c Veronika Surovtseva/Thinkstock; 68b DutchScenery/Thinkstock; 68e Milan Maksic/Thinkstock; 68d hxdyl/iStockphoto; 69a AndreAnita/iStockphotos; 69b Oskari Porkka/iStockphotos; 69c vencavolrab/Thinkstock; 70a vladvvm/Thinkstock; 70b elnavegante/iStockphoto; 70c ©Ruth Black| Dreamstime.com; 71a ©Svetlana Kuznetsova|Dreamstime.com; 71d ©Monkey Business Images Ltd| Dreamstime.com; 71c Png-Studio/iStockphotos; 71b JuSun/istockphotos; 72c leonello/iStock; 72d janscherders/iStock; 72b mycola/iStock; 72a ©Piksel|Dreamstime.com; 74a Yoyochow23/Thinkstock; 74b Devonyu/Thinkstock; 74c cherezoff/Thinkstock; 74d bhidethescene/Thinkstock; 74e Coprid/Thinkstock; 74f Coprid/Thinkstock; 75p leeview/Thinkstock; 76a Sergey Peterman/Thinkstock; 76b neamov/Thinkstock; 76c McAndy/Thinkstock; 76d sunstock/Thinkstock; 76e iStock; 76f JackF/Thinkstock; 76g David De Lossy Thinkstock; 76h Monkey Business Images/Thinkstock; 77a Miroslaw Kijewski/Thinkstock; 77b GlobalP/Thinkstock; 77c Andy Lidstone/Thinkstock; 77d Nneirda/Thinkstock; 77e tonivaver/Thinkstock; 77f Obalazs/Thinkstock; 79a Epicstock/Dreamstime.com; 79b John Howard/Thinkstock; 79c GaleVerhague/Dreamstime.com; 79d FogStock/Vico Images/Alin Dragulin/Thinkstock; 83a BrianAJackson/Thinkstock ; 83b JacekChabraszewski/iStockphoto; 83c Noel Hendrickson/Thinkstock; 83d barsik/Thinkstock; 86a monkeybusinessimages/iStockphoto; 86b DragonImages/Dreamstime.com; 87a ISTOCK; 87b JungleOutThere/Thinkstock; 87c Nerthuz/Thinkstock; 88a Erwin Purnomosidi/Thinkstock; 88b EkaterinaMinaeva/Thinkstock; 88c Christine Korten|Dreamstime.com; 88d SergZSV/Thinkstock; 90a Jupiterimages/Thinkstock; 90b Purestock/Thinkstock; 91a CoffmanCMU/iStockphoto; 91b Milan Maksic/Thinkstock; 91c Andreea Florian/Dreamstime.com; 91d nicholashan/iStockphoto; 91e Sayhmog/iStockphoto; 91f hxdyl/iStockphoto; 91g Picsfive/Thinkstock; 91h OLEKSANDR PEREPELYTSIA/Thinkstock; 91g Lalouetto/Thinkstock; 93 ©Ralf Kraft|Dreamstime.com; 94 colorcocktail/Thinkstock; 96a SergeiKorolko/Thinkstock; 96b Askold Romanov/Thinkstock; 96c frenkvic/Thinkstock; 96d Route55/Thinkstock; 96e Macrovector/Dreamstime.com; 96f Ijansempoi/Dreamstime.com; 96g Olga Popova/Dreamstime.com; 96hPixelrobot/Dreamstime.com96i Maxim Garagulin/Dreamstime.com97/98Mark Evans/iStockphoto99a Ryan McVay/Thinkstock; 99b Mark Evans/iStockphoto; 99c nabihariahi/Thinkstock; 99d Thinkstock; 99e neskez/Thinkstock; 101 ©imageBROKER/Alamy Stock Photo; 102 IuriiSokolov/Thinkstock; 103a tiler84/Thinkstock; 103b richwai777/Thinkstock; 103c Siri Stafford/Thinkstock; 103d TomLeGoff/Thinkstock; 103e moodboard/Thinkstock; 103f skaylim/Thinkstock; 103g Romariolen/Thinkstock; 103h KatarzynaBialasiewicz/Thinkstock; 104a 3D_generator/Thinkstock; 104b maxkabakov/Thinkstock; 104c BananaStock/Thinkstock; 104d AnnBaldwin/Thinkstock; 105a yamahavalerossi/Thinkstock105b; Grzegorz Petrykowski/Thinkstock; 105 crimglow/Thinkstock; 105d ozgurkeser/Thinkstock; 106a 0; 106b BrianMcEntire/Thinkstock; 106c

Artranq/Thinkstock; **106d** fruta - shironosov/Thinkstock; **107a** AnnBaldwin/Thinkstock; **107b** Tom Le Goff/Thinkstock; **107c** macky_ch/Thinkstock; **107d** Jani Bryson/Thinkstock; **107e** Karmeel/Thinkstock; **107f** Milan Markovic/Thinkstock; **107g** ilona75/Thinkstock; **108a** moodboard/Thinkstock; **108b** Staas/Thinkstock; **108c** shvili/Thinkstock; **108d** stockstudio/Thinkstock; **109a** © Buddha13|Dreamstime.com; **109b/c/d** Danielrao/iStock Photo; **113** lisafx/Thinkstock; **116a** acidgrey/Thinkstock; **116b**/dgresei/Thinkstock; **116e** thawats/Thinkstock; **116f** GlobalP/Thinkstock; **116c** geniebird/Thinkstock; **116g** Henrik_L/Thinkstock; **116h** adogslifephoto/Thinkstock; **117a** ©Valentin Armianu|Dreamstime.com; **117b** Jason Edwards/Getty Images; **117c** © Mike P Shepherd/AlamyStockPhoto; **118a** LeeYiuTung/Thinkstock; **118b** RobinEriksson/Thinkstock; **118c** USO/Thinkstock; **118d** Sunheyy/Dreamstime.com; **118e** Imphilip/Dreamstime.com; **118f** Volodymyr Byrdyak/Dreamstime.com; **119a** Paul Hart/Thinkstock; **119b** atese/Thinkstock; **119c** vadimfogel/Thinkstock; **119d** Vasilvich/Thinkstock; **119e** Cucu Remus/Thinkstock; **119f** vs_lt/Thinkstock; **119g** Medioimages/Photodisc/Thinkstock; **120a** karamysh/Thinkstock; **120b** JLKoons/Thinkstock; **120c** DAJ/Thinkstock; **121a** mosca - Purestock/Thinkstock; **121b** itasun/Thinkstock; **121c** Daniela Bethke/Thinkstock; **122a** GlobalP/Thinkstock; **122b** tolisma/Thinkstock; **122c** karandaev/Thinkstock; **122d** GlobalP/Thinkstock; **122e** K_attapon/Thinkstock; **122f** AndrisTkachenko/Thinkstock; **122g** adogslifephoto/Thinkstock; **122h** lindavostrovska/Thinkstock; **122i** OxfordSquare/Thinkstock; **123a** gbh007/Thinkstock; **123b** GlobalP/Thinkstock; **123c** vitalytitov/Thinkstock; **126a** Antonio_Diaz/Thinkstock; **126b** Ingram Publishing/Thinkstock; **127a** kindi/Dreamstime.com; **127b** monkeybusinessimages/Thinkstock; **128a** Getty Images/Thinkstock; **128b** LuminaStock/Thinkstock; **128c** Halfpoint/Thinkstock; **128d** Creatas/Thinkstock; **129a** IPGGutenbergUKLtd/Thinkstock; **130a** MR1805/Thinkstock; **130b** MR1805/Thinkstock; **133a** rep0rter/Thinkstock; **133b** AFP PHOTO /SPC; **136a** dolgachov/istock; **137a** Thomas Northcut/Thinkstock; **137b** sewer11/Thinkstock; **137c** Supertruper/Thinkstock; **137d** vidalidali/Thinkstock; **137e** Evgeny Sergeev/Thinkstock; **140a** © Rawpixelimages | Dreamstime.com

All other images © Pearson Education

Every effort has been made to trace the copyright holders and we apologise in advance for any unintentional omissions or incorrect citations. We would be pleased to insert the appropriate acknowledgement in any subsequent edition of this publication

Notes

Notes

Notes

Notes